SNOWDON

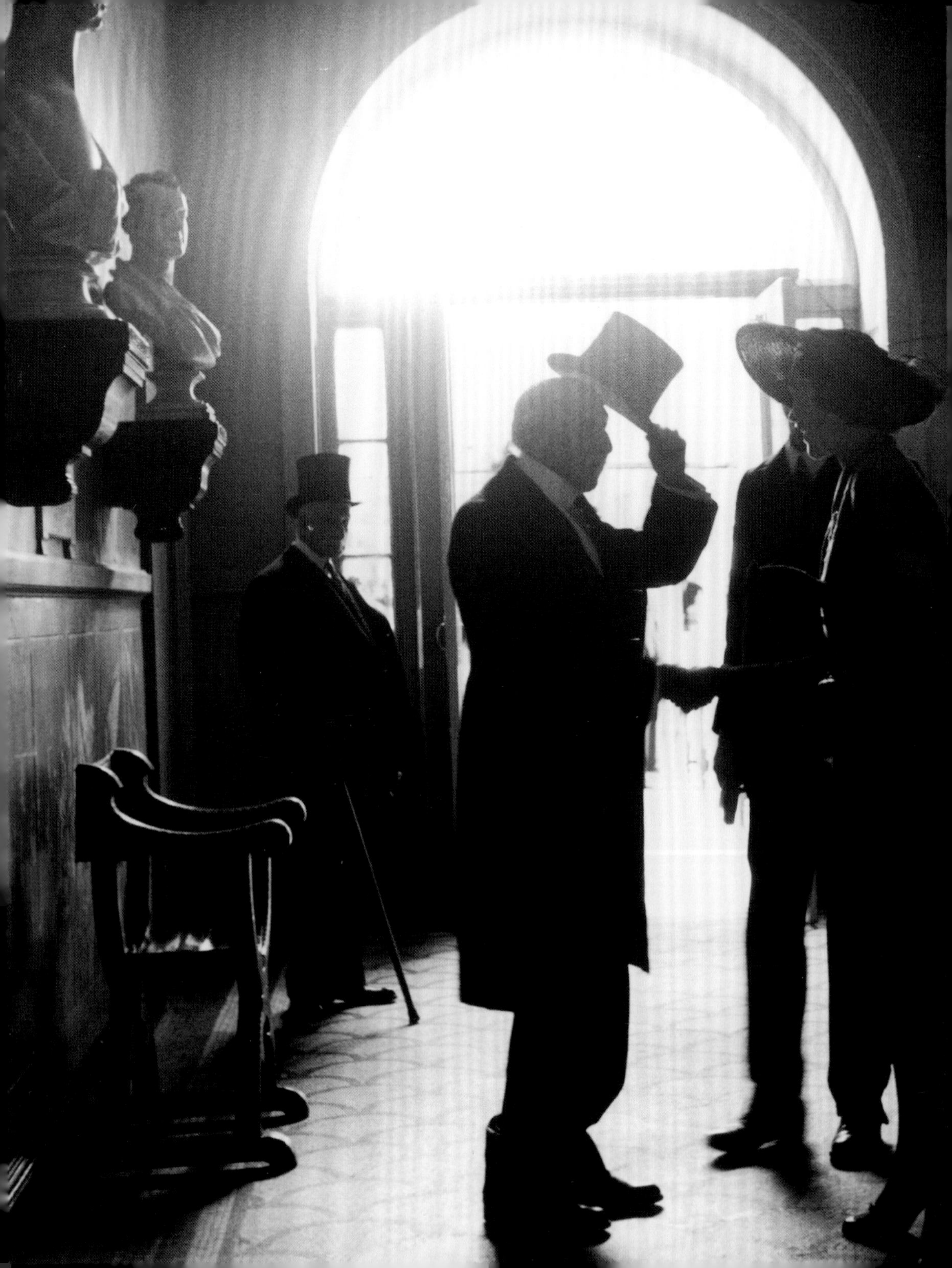

SNOWDON

CHRIS BEETLES GALLERY

8 & 10 Ryder Street   St. James's   London SW1Y 6QB

TELEPHONE 0207 839 7551   FAX 0207 839 1603   EMAIL gallery@chrisbeetles.com   WEB www.chrisbeetles.com

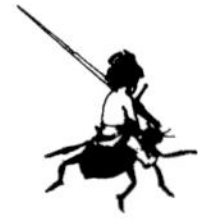

Images © 2006 Lord Snowdon,
archive represented by Camera Press, London

Chris Beetles Gallery
8 & 10 Ryder Street
London
SW1Y 6QB

Telephone 0207 839 7551
Fax 0207 839 1603
E-mail gallery@chrisbeetles.com
Website www.chrisbeetles.com

ISBN 1 871136 99 7

Edited and compiled by GILES HUXLEY-PARLOUR
Design by THE BRIDGEWATER BOOK COMPANY
Colour separation and printing by BAS PRINTERS

CONTENTS

INTRODUCTION

A studio shoot with Lord Snowdon is quite often an uncomfortable experience. He has an uncanny ability to see through even the toughest facades, to strip pretensions, and by removing whatever pride his sitters arrive with, reveal the truth. Although famous for his charm and perfect manners, he likes to unnerve. This approach, coupled with his instinct to press the shutter at *exactly* the right moment, has made him a world famous photographer.

Despite this well-honed, well-known technique he has no recognisable photographic style, and indeed for the last half-century has made efforts to avoid developing one. He feels that as a photographer his role is to become an invisible observer, coaxing the truth out of his subjects without turning the result into a 'Snowdon'. Sifting through the thousands of photographs that we reduced to the representative selection in this catalogue, it became clear just how very different his work can appear as a result. He is a master of studio portraiture, photo-journalism, theatre, fashion, advertising, travel, nature and even underwater photography. His versatility is enormous; the ultimate photographic polymath.

Antony Armstrong-Jones was born in 1930, and seemed destined for a career in the arts; it was in his blood after all. His great-grandfather was the Punch cartoonist and photographer Linley Sambourne

(1845-1910), and his uncle was the legendary theatre, ballet and opera designer Oliver Messel (1904-1978). Indeed, his prep-school headmaster guessed that academia was not his thing reporting; 'Armstrong–Jones may be good at something, but it's nothing that we teach here.'

His first forays into photography were at Eton, where he revived the Photographic Society and at Cambridge where he was a regular contributor to the *Varsity* magazine. Armstrong-Jones moved to London and after two apprenticeships, opened his own studio in a converted ironmonger's shop in 1952. From this Pimlico base he began to forge the beginnings of a reputation. His pictures were being featured in *Tatler* and he got his first spread in the *Picture Post*; flamenco dancers at an Oliver Messel party. He also began to photograph the theatre, starting with the 1954 production of Terence Rattigan's *Separate Tables*. The approach that he took was unheard of at the time, and was soon to establish his name. Disregarding the tradition for highly organised, posed pieces taken with large format, plate cameras, he chose to use a miniature camera to get amongst the actors backstage and during rehearsal, in an attempt to capture the essence of the play. The best results of this technique are badly lit, grainy, blurred and unusually composed. They deliberately reject traditional photographic values, brim with atmosphere, and embody the rebellious, vigorous energy that swept through British theatre in the 1950s. A picture in this style of Alec Guinness taken during a rehearsal of *Hotel Paradiso* first caught the attention of theatreland, and Armstrong-Jones was thereafter the photographer of choice for actors, directors and producers at this radically exciting time.

By 1956 he was already branching out beyond portraiture and theatre, working on advertising and fashion shoots for *Tatler, Vogue, Harper's Bazaar,* and *The Daily Express*, and beginning to research a book that was to be called simply, *London*. This was published in 1958 by Weidenfeld and Nicholson, and is a portrait of a city that takes the reader from seedy strip joints in Canning Town to The Chelsea Flower Show and The Trooping of the Colour. His pictures concentrate on the people of London rather than the buildings, and illustrate his interest in human interplay, reactions and expressions over formal composition and polish. His strong journalistic bent, so relied upon by newspapers in the decades to come, is obvious. *London* began a list of books now twenty-two strong, the latest being of India, published in Autumn 2006 by the Khemka Foundation.

Armstrong-Jones's marriage to Princess Margaret in 1960 slowed down his so far meteoric photographic career. Following the birth of their son, David, in 1960, he was created 1st Earl of Snowdon and spent much of his time performing royal duties. However, he still made time to do shoots for *The Sunday Times* colour supplement. In 1962 for example, he embarked on a series of touching pictures examining old age, finally published in 1965, the first of a number of commissions that dealt with social issues. He photographed a fourteen page article on British theatre in 1966 that coined the phrase 'swinging London', and he travelled to India, Japan and Italy for the magazine at various points during the decade. Although his photographic career slowed down, it gave him the freedom to indulge in other creative pursuits. From 1960 to 1965 he was commissioned to design a new aviary for London Zoo. The project, now a grade II listed building, took five years to complete and remains one of Snowdon's proudest achievements. He won two Emmys for a television documentary, *Don't Count the Candles* in 1968, and was also made responsible for the overall design of the investiture of the Prince of Wales in 1969.

By 1970 he was back working for *Vogue*, back working at the level of intensity that suited his drive, and was one of the most in-demand photographers in the country. His output from the decade is huge; he made six television documentaries, published seven books of his own work, held exhibitions in Cologne, London, the Far East, and Australia, whilst all the time contributing to the publications he helped define. This tireless attitude to work has continued to the present day. Now aged seventy six he has problems walking due to boyhood polio, but still holds regular shoots at the remarkably small and unpretentious home studio in which many of his photographs were taken, most recently the 80th birthday portrait of the Queen. The National Portrait Gallery, which holds one hundred and seventeen of his pictures, held a retrospective show in 2000 that toured to Edinburgh, Vienna, Moscow and the Yale Centre for British Art in the United States. He has published four books since turning seventy, still travels extensively, and refuses point-blank to bask in the indelible reputation that he has worked hard at since 1952. This is his first ever selling show.

GILES HUXLEY-PARLOUR

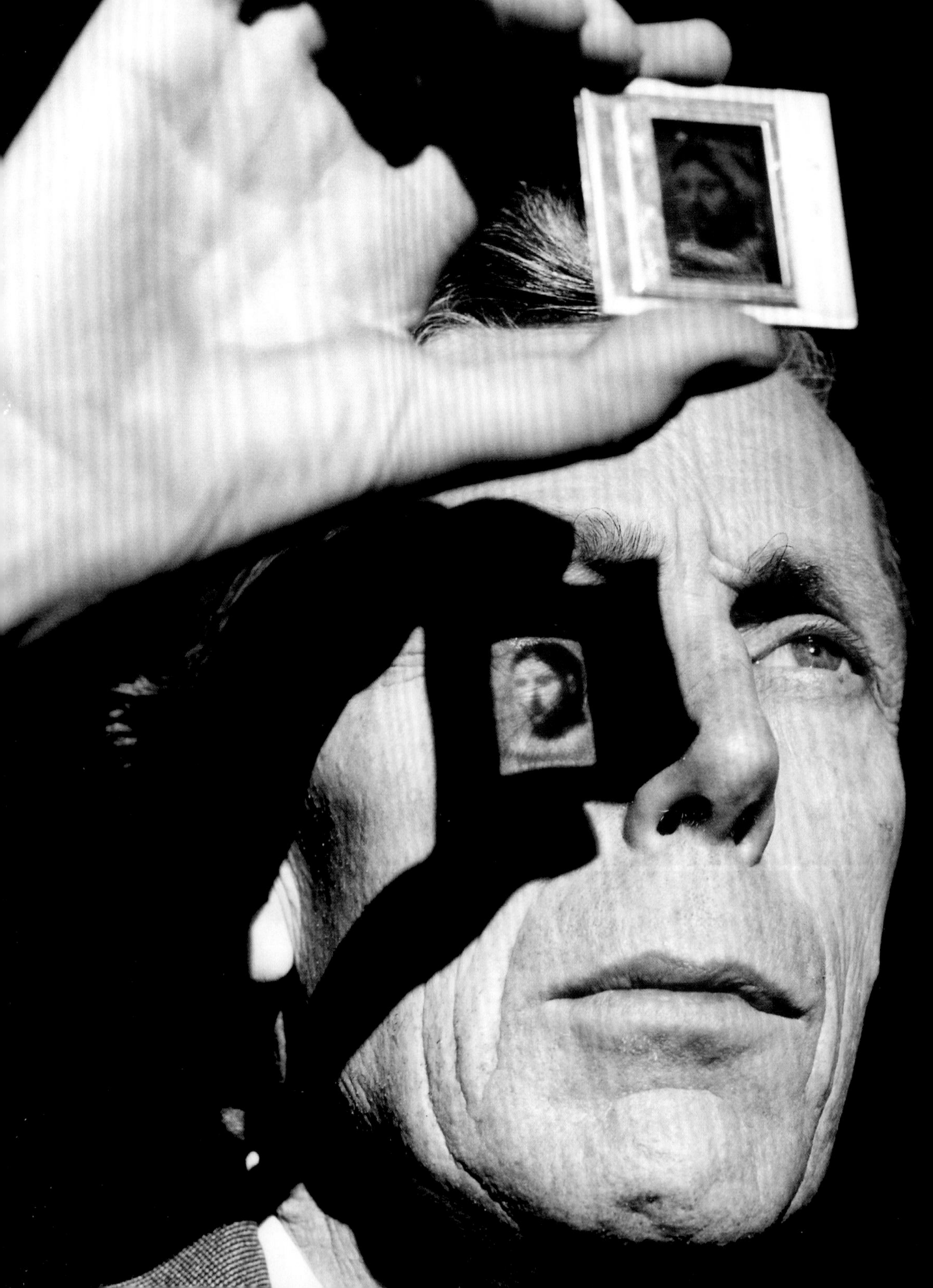

PLATES

12

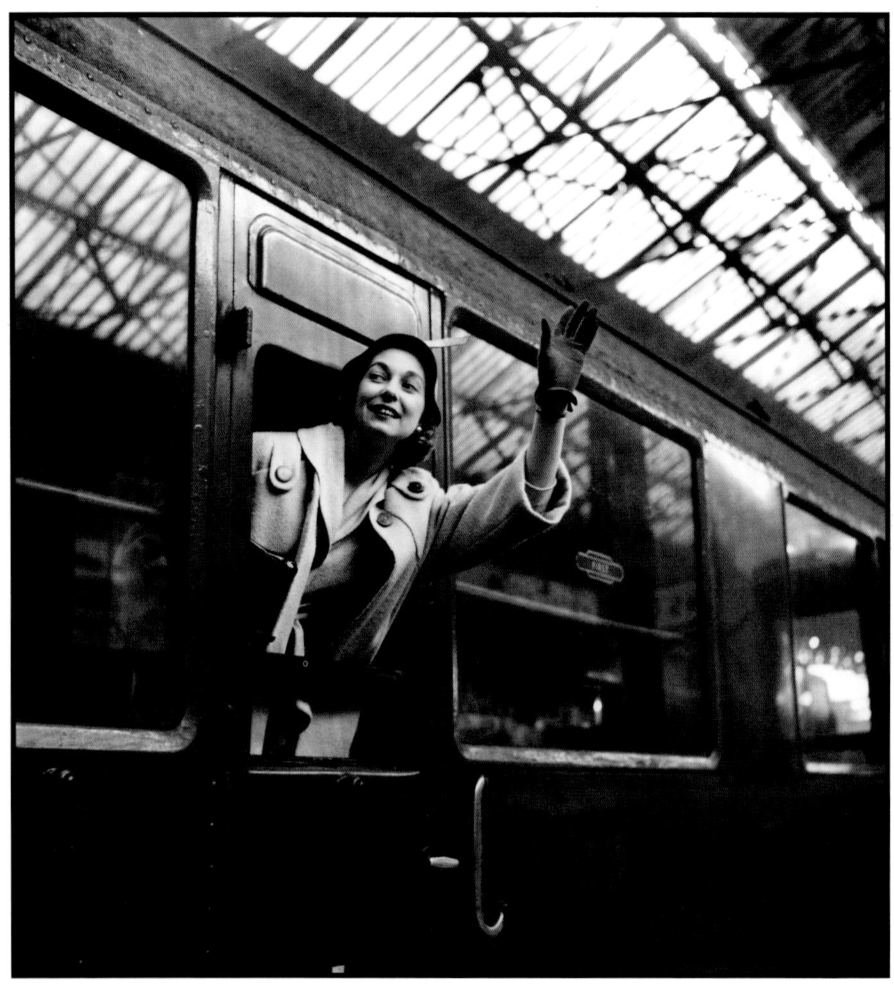

1

GLORIA CLARRY IN A *TATLER* FASHION SPREAD

1955

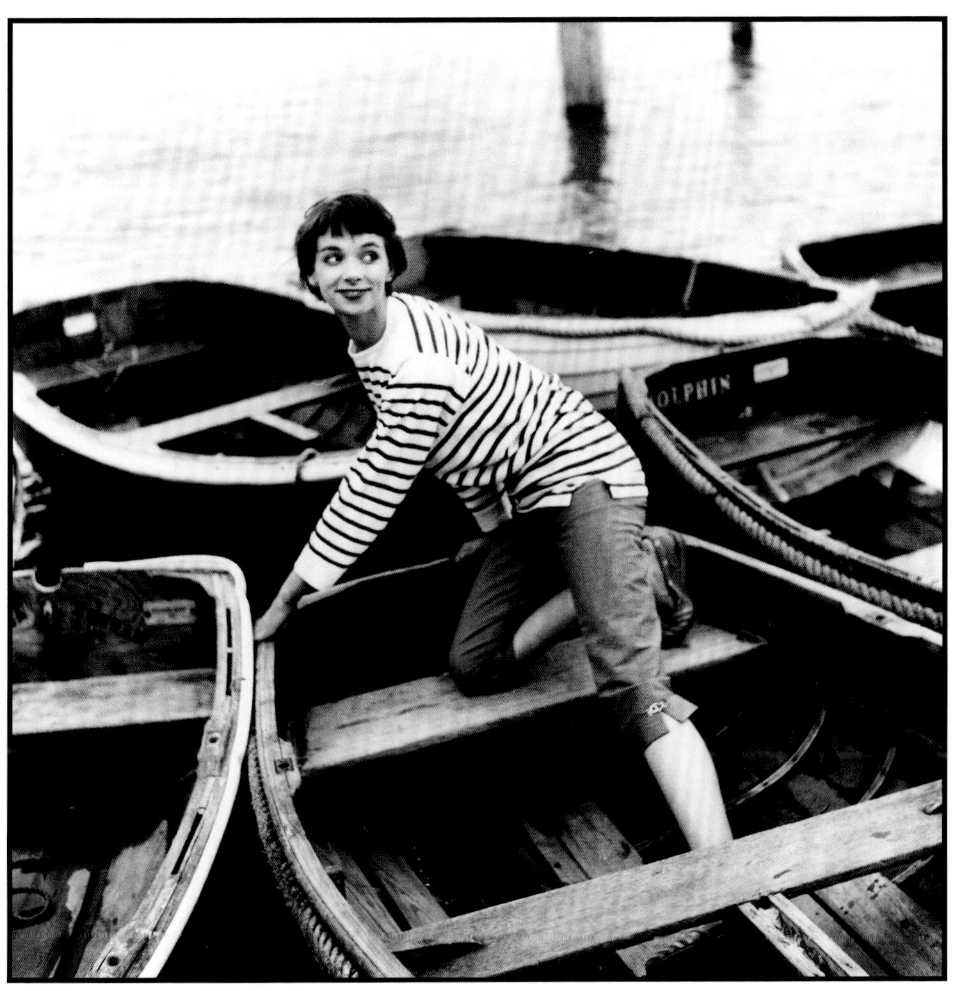

2

GRETA WATSON IN A *TATLER* FASHION SPREAD
1955

14

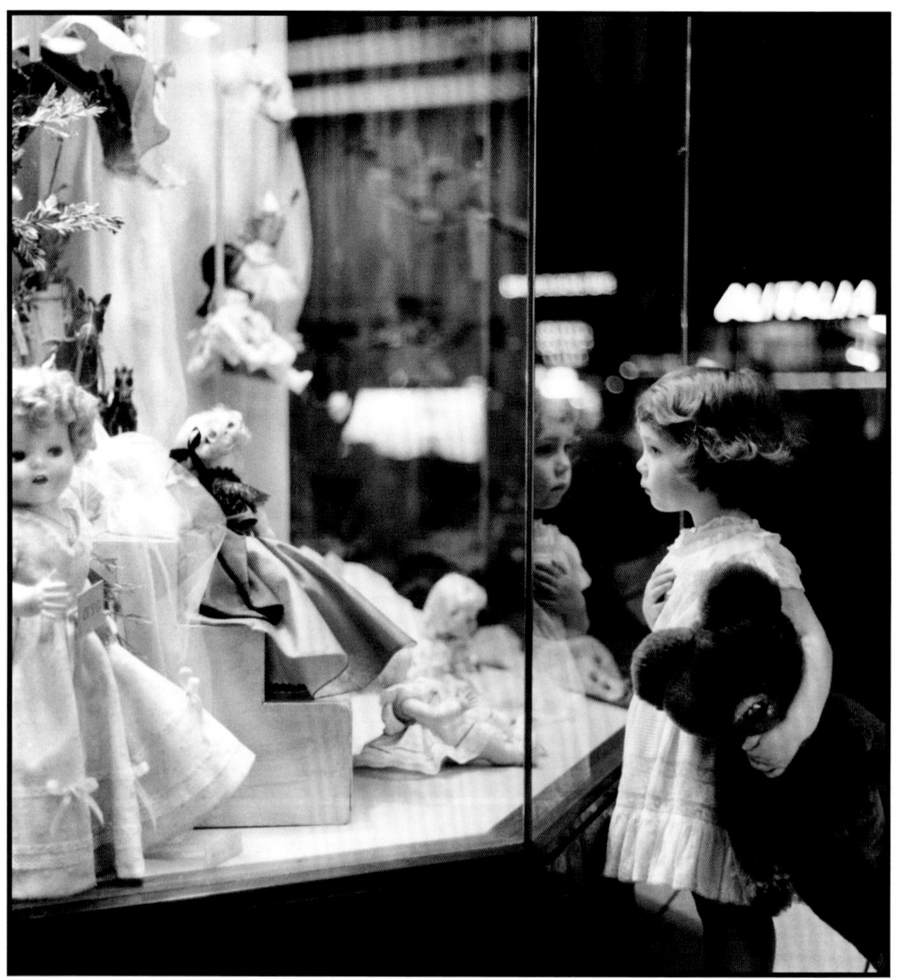

3
—

ADVERTISEMENT FOR HAMLEY'S TOYS
1956

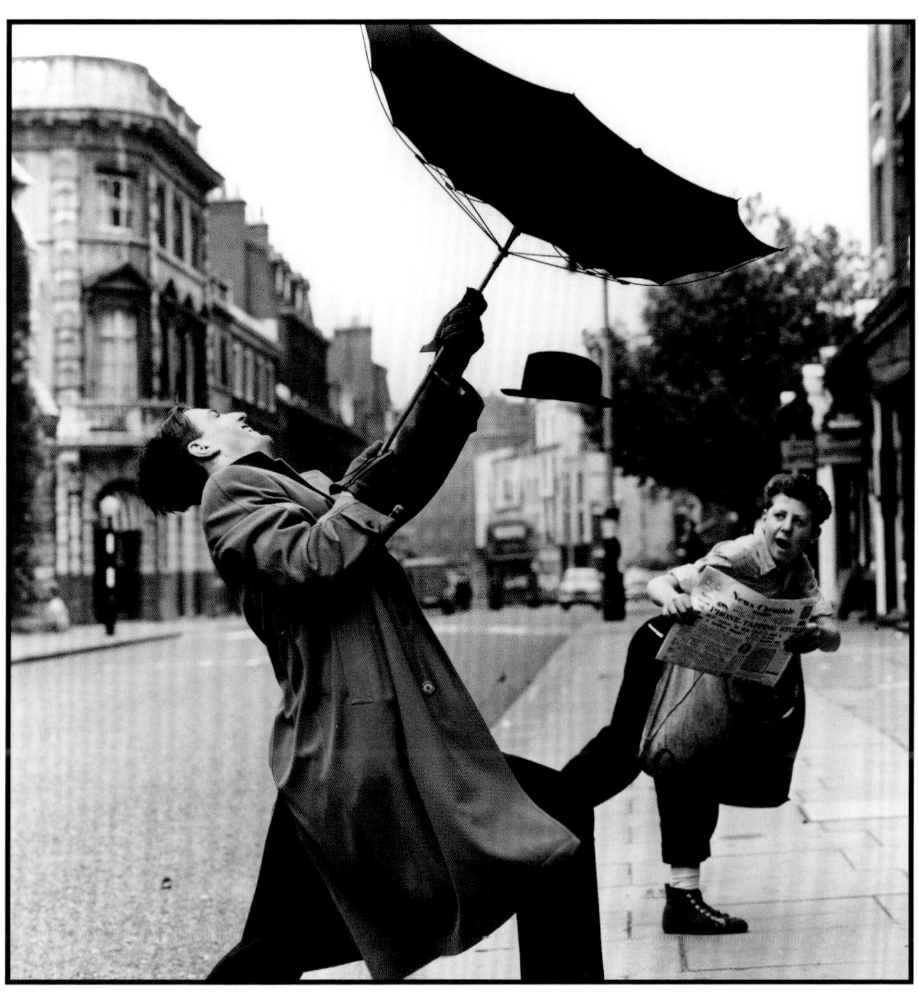

15

4

ROBIN TATERSAL IN AN ADVERTISEMENT FOR ACRILAN

1957

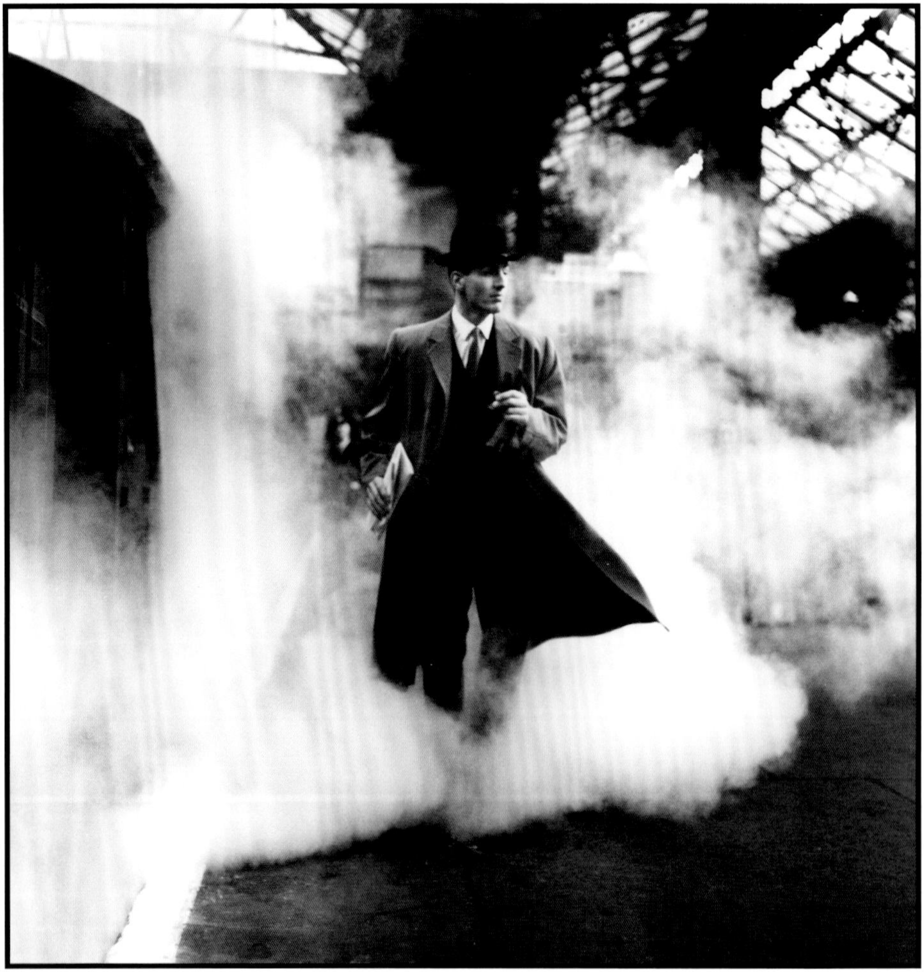

16

5

ROBIN TATERSAL IN AN ADVERTISEMENT FOR ACRILAN

1957

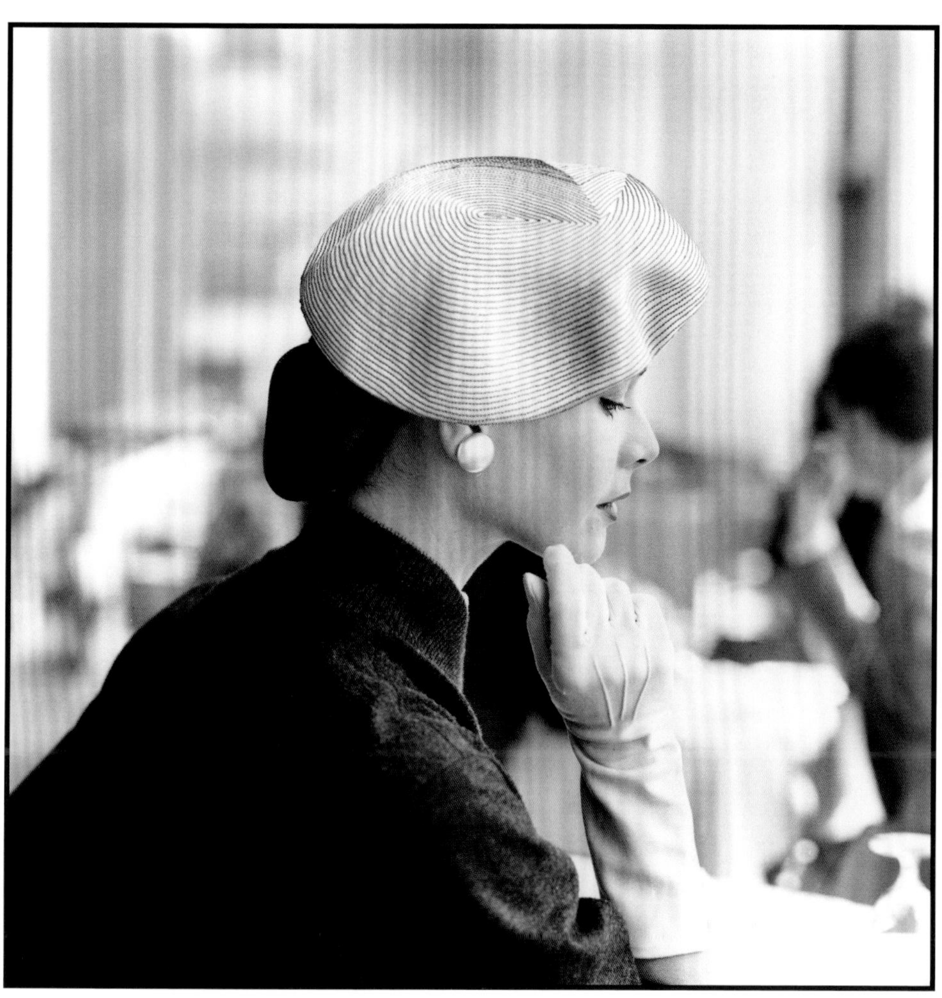

6

JEAN QUICK IN AN ADVERTISEMENT FOR COURTAULDS HATS

1957

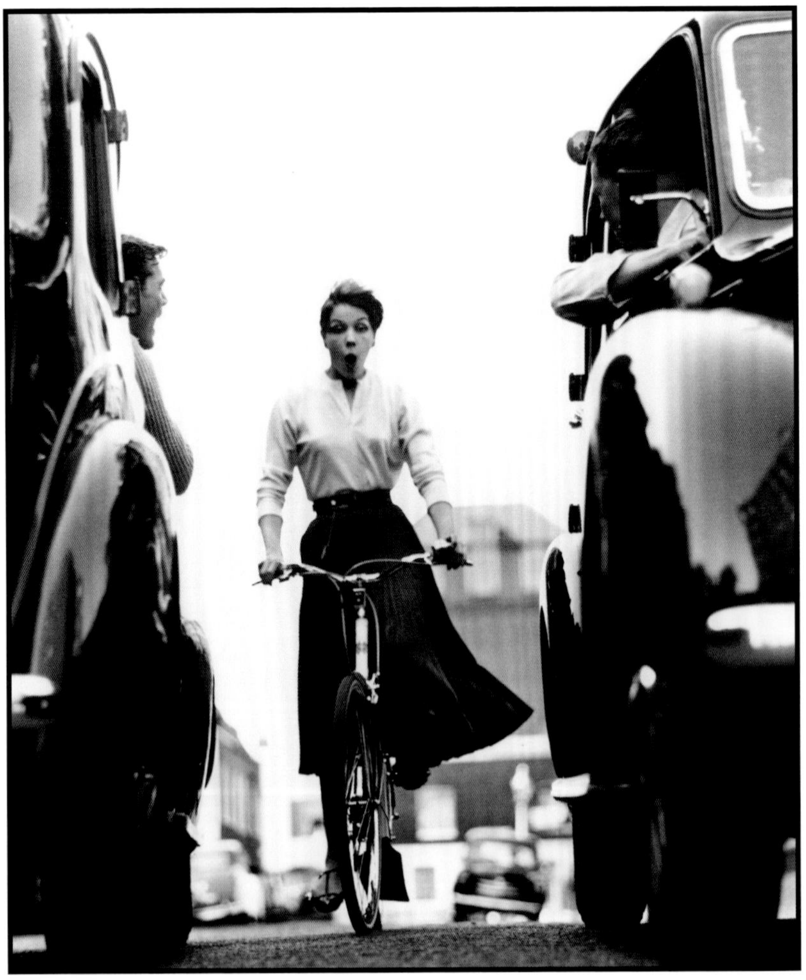

7

ACRILAN ADVERTISEMENT
1957

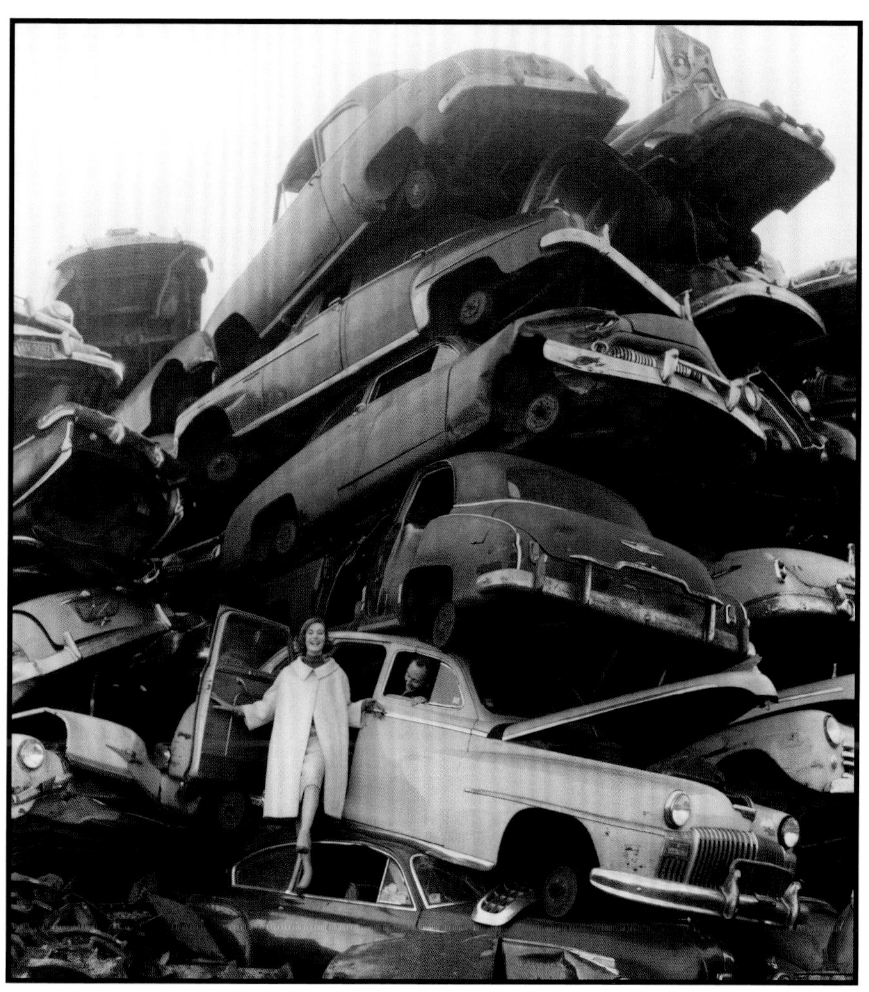

19

8

FASHION STILL, JUNKYARD, QUEENS, NEW YORK
1957

20

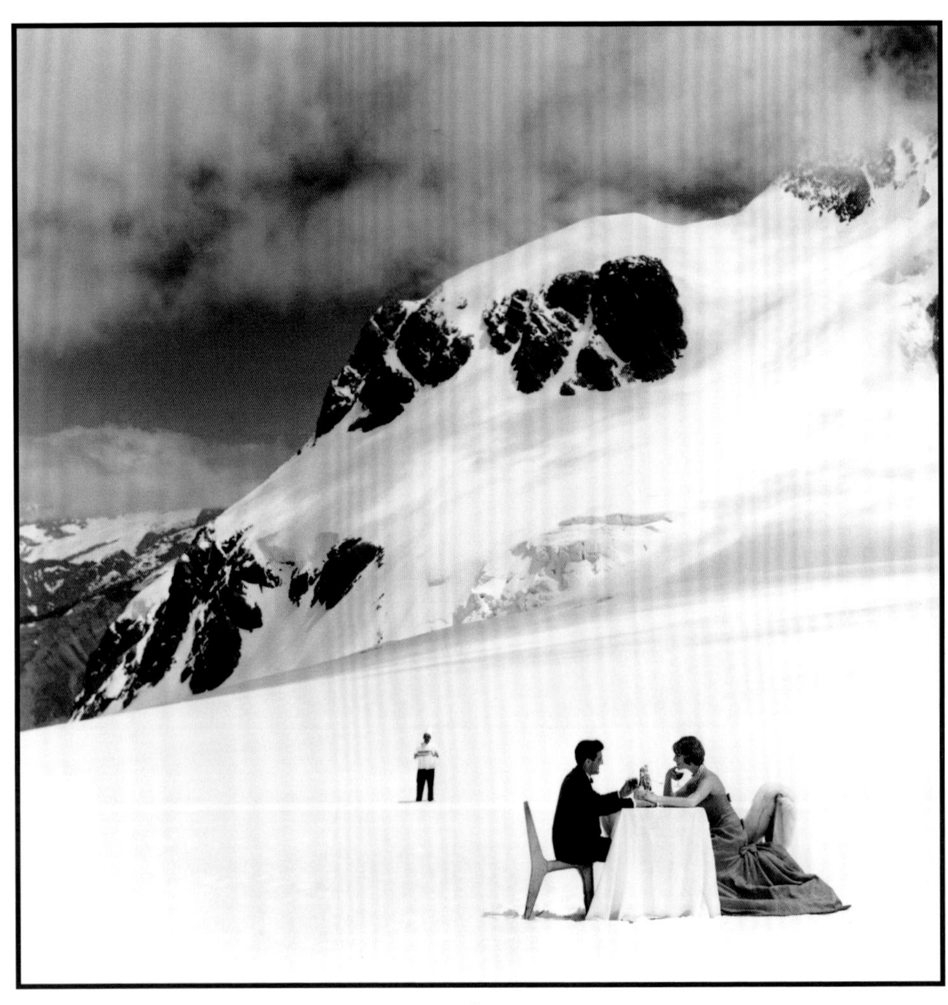

9

SEKERS SILK ADVERTISEMENT, CERVINIA, ITALY
1958

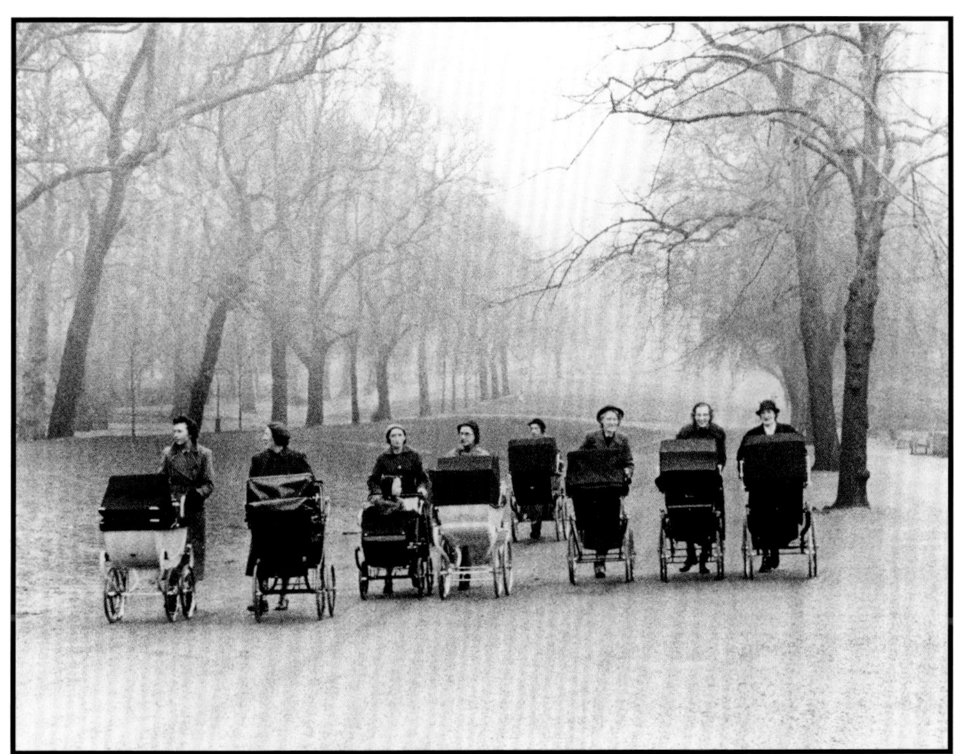

10

NANNIES ON ROTTEN ROW, LONDON
1958

22

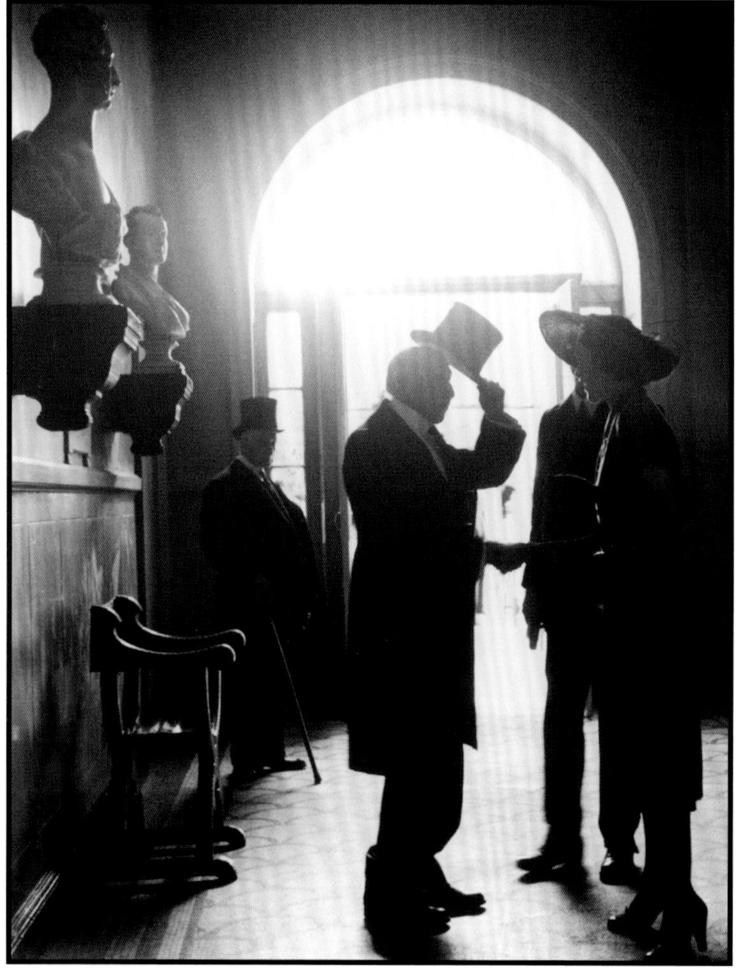

11
—

MR WILLIAM STONE, ALBANY, PICCADILLY, LONDON
1953

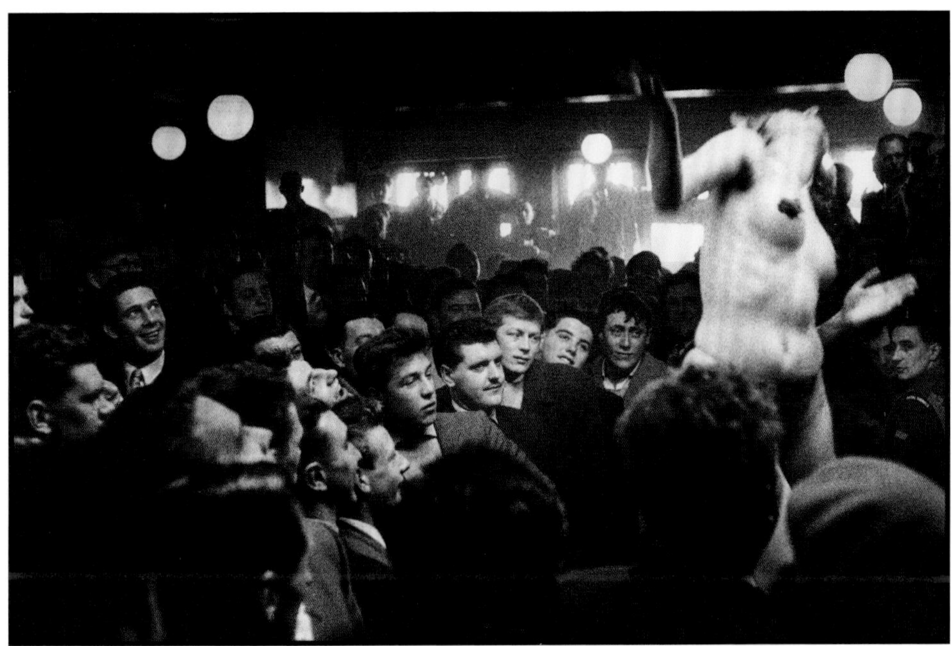

12

SUNDAY LUNCH AT THE BRIDGEHOUSE HOTEL, CANNING TOWN, LONDON

1958

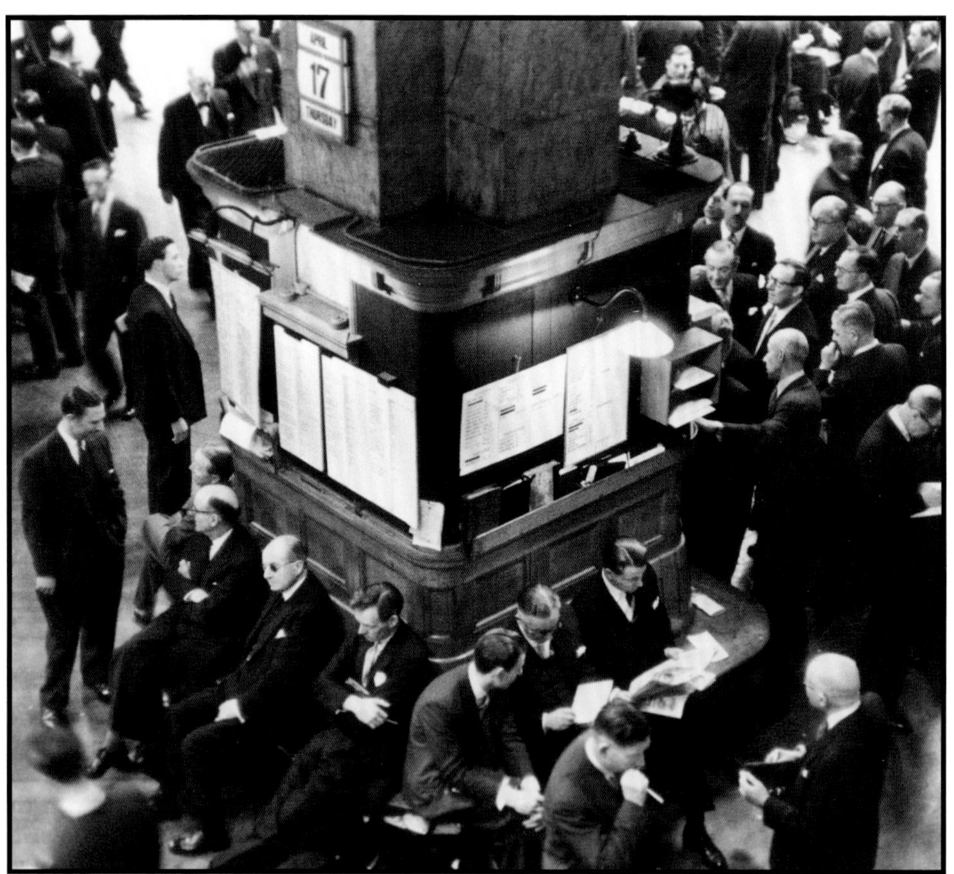

24

13
—

THE LONDON STOCK EXCHANGE, LONDON
1958

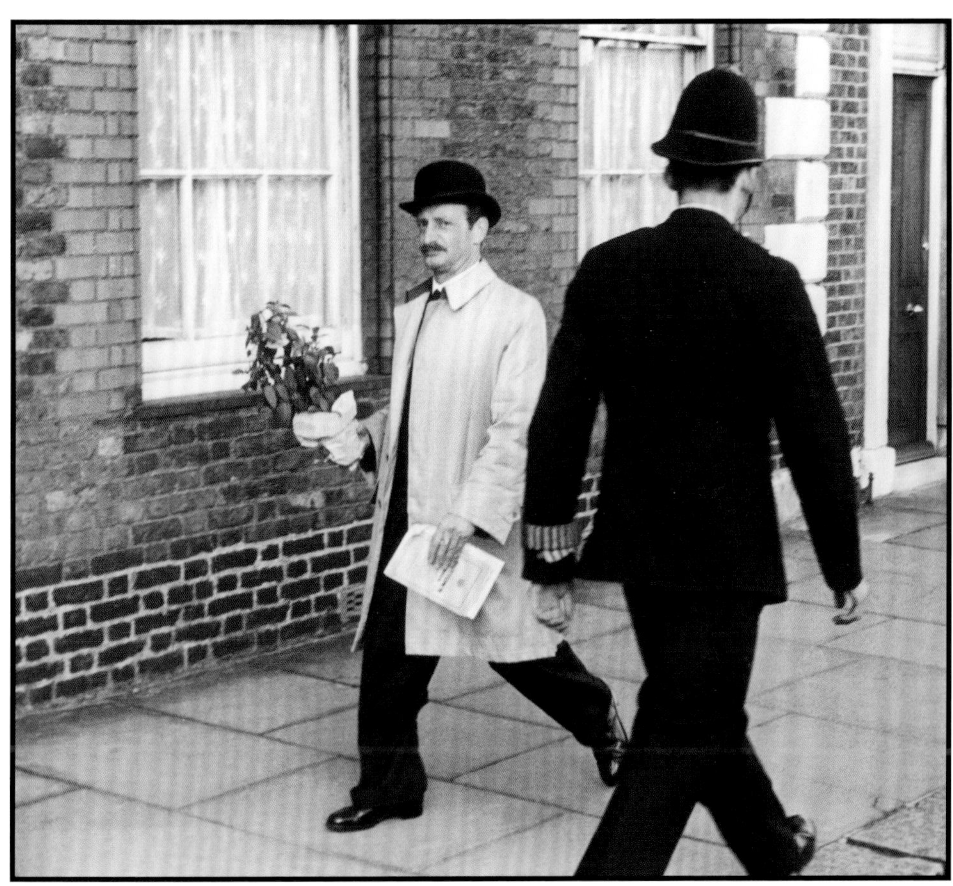

14

LAST DAY OF THE CHELSEA FLOWER SHOW, LONDON

1958

26

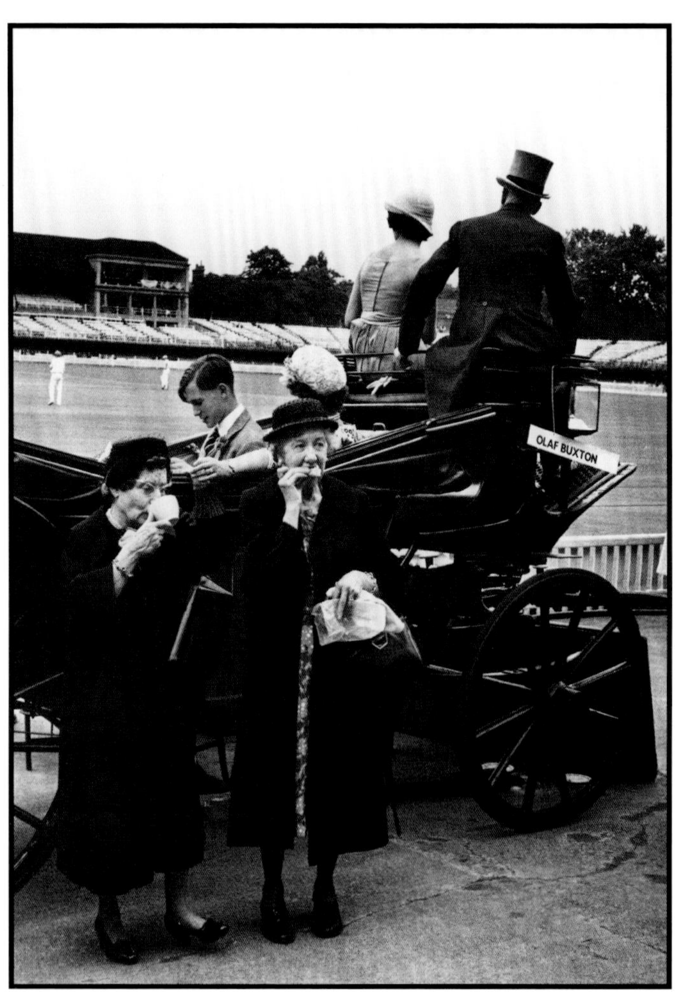

15
—

THE ETON AND HARROW CRICKET MATCH, LORDS, LONDON
1958

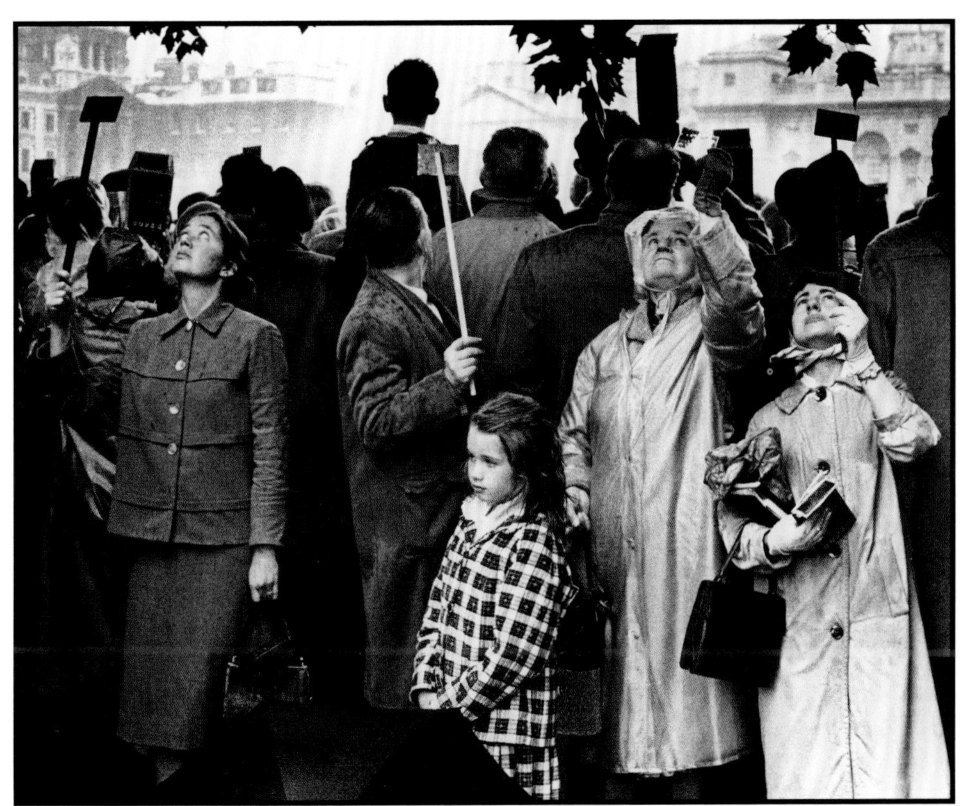

27

16

TROOPING THE COLOUR, LONDON
1958

28

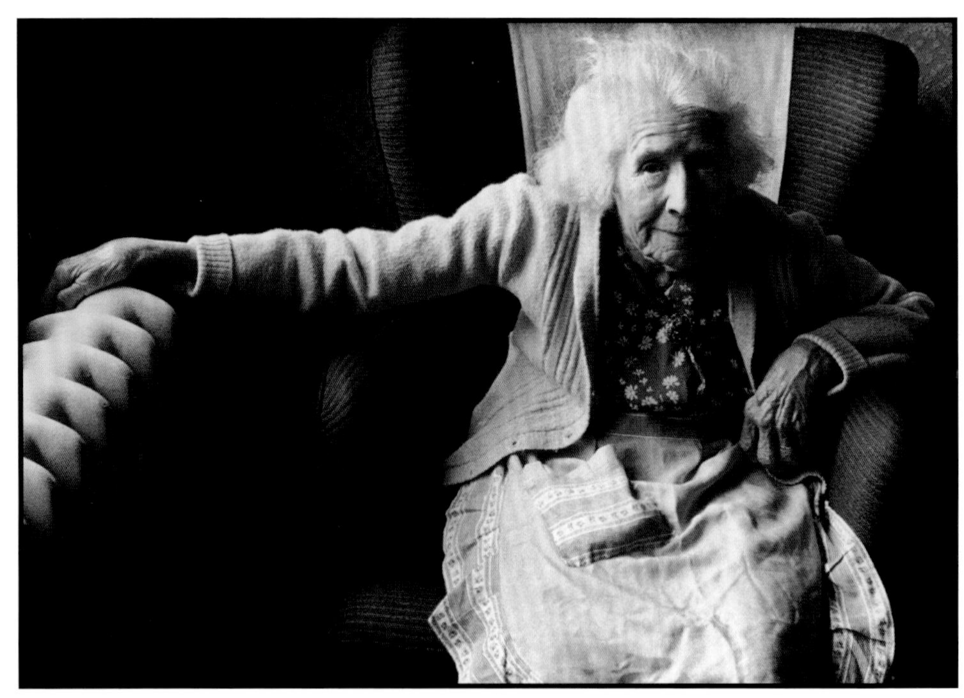

17
—

OLD AGE, *THE SUNDAY TIMES MAGAZINE*
1964

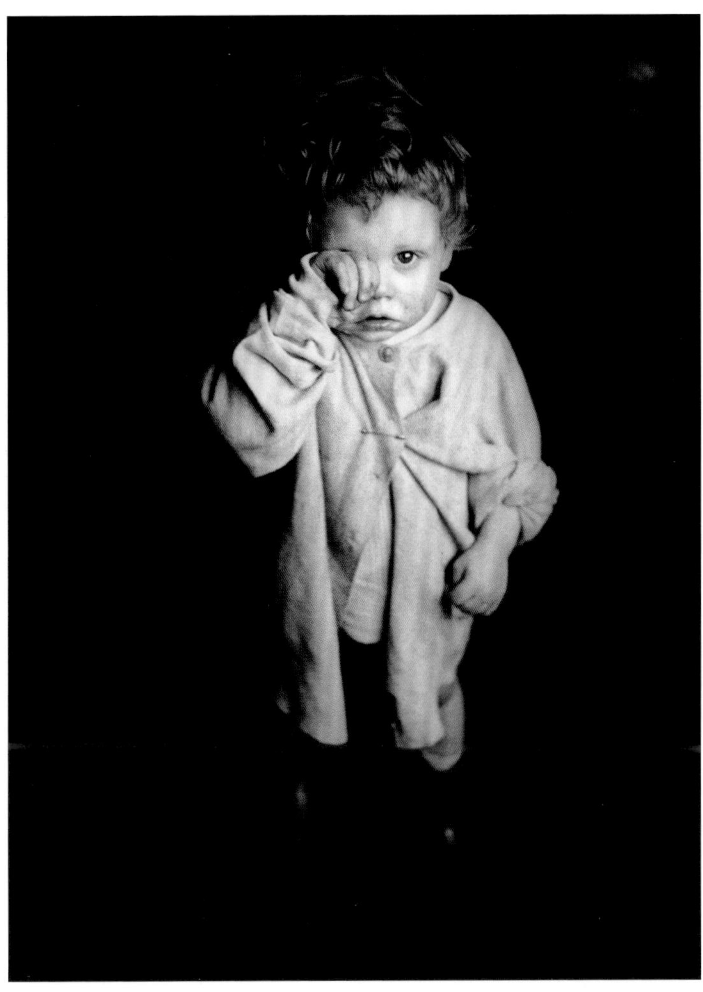

18

SOME OF OUR CHILDREN, *THE SUNDAY TIMES MAGAZINE*
1965

30

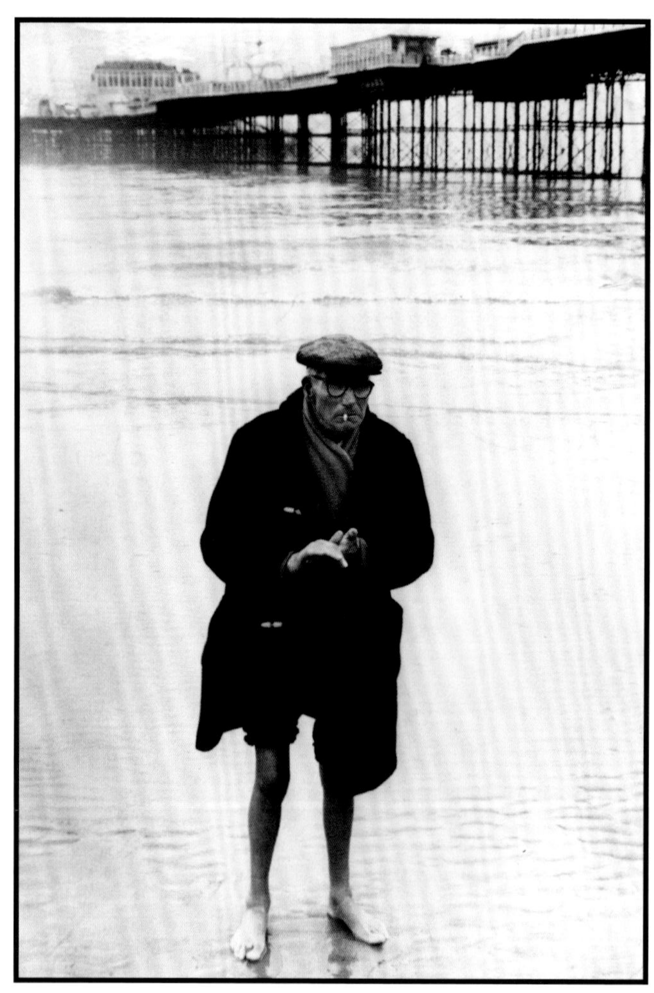

19
—
LONELINESS (DEAF MUTE IN BRIGHTON),
THE SUNDAY TIMES MAGAZINE
1966

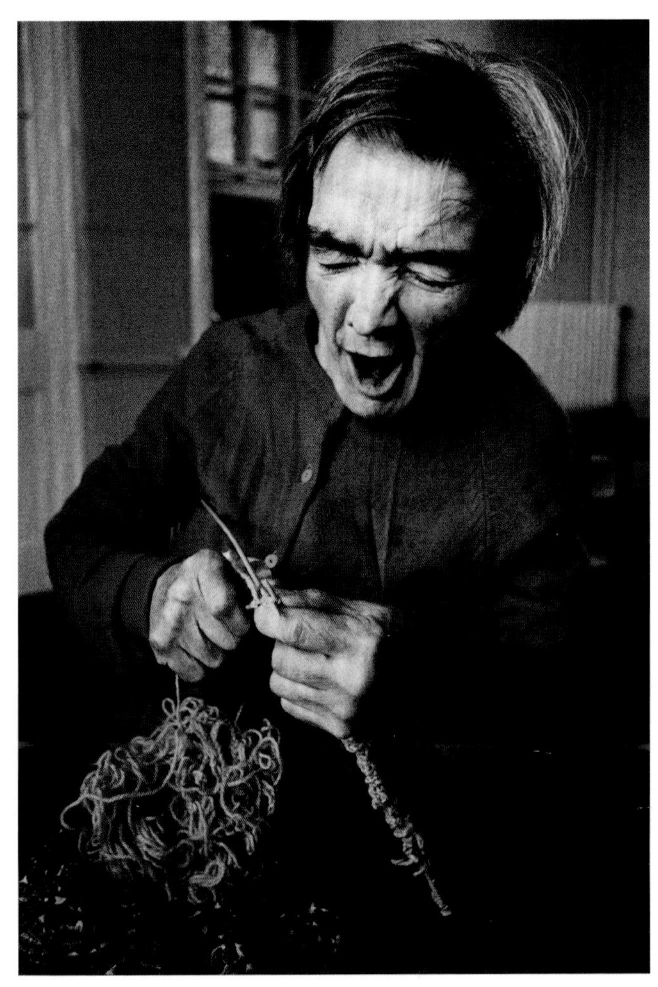

20

MENTAL HOSPITALS (PATIENT KNITTING),
THE SUNDAY TIMES MAGAZINE
1968

32

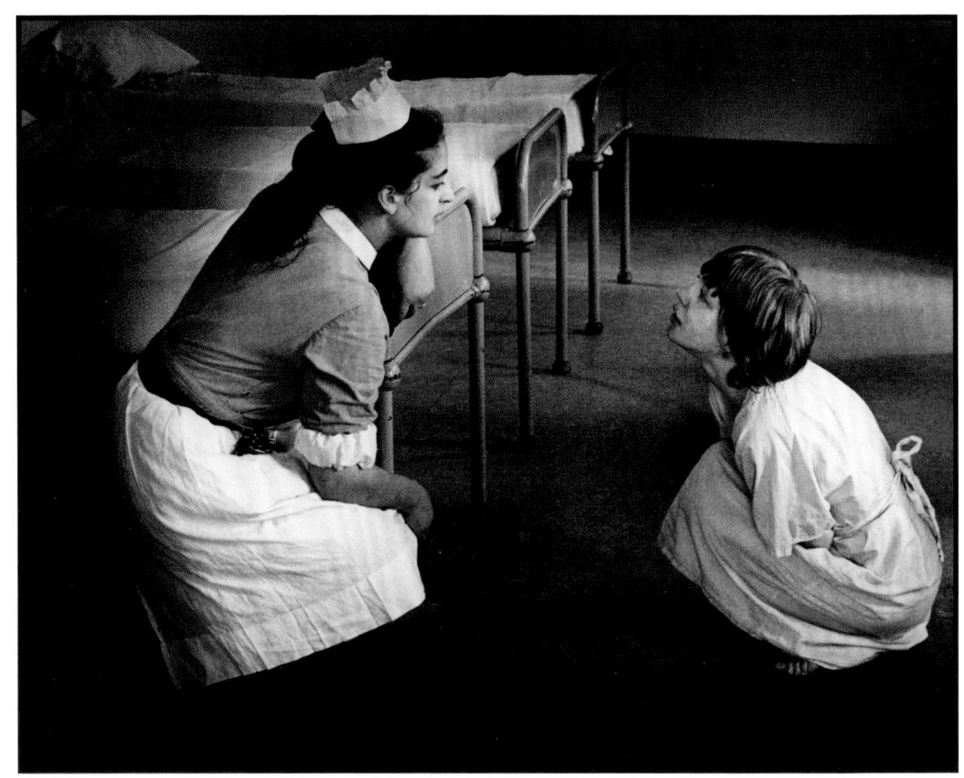

21
—

MENTAL HOSPITALS (NURSE AND PATIENT),
THE SUNDAY TIMES MAGAZINE
1968

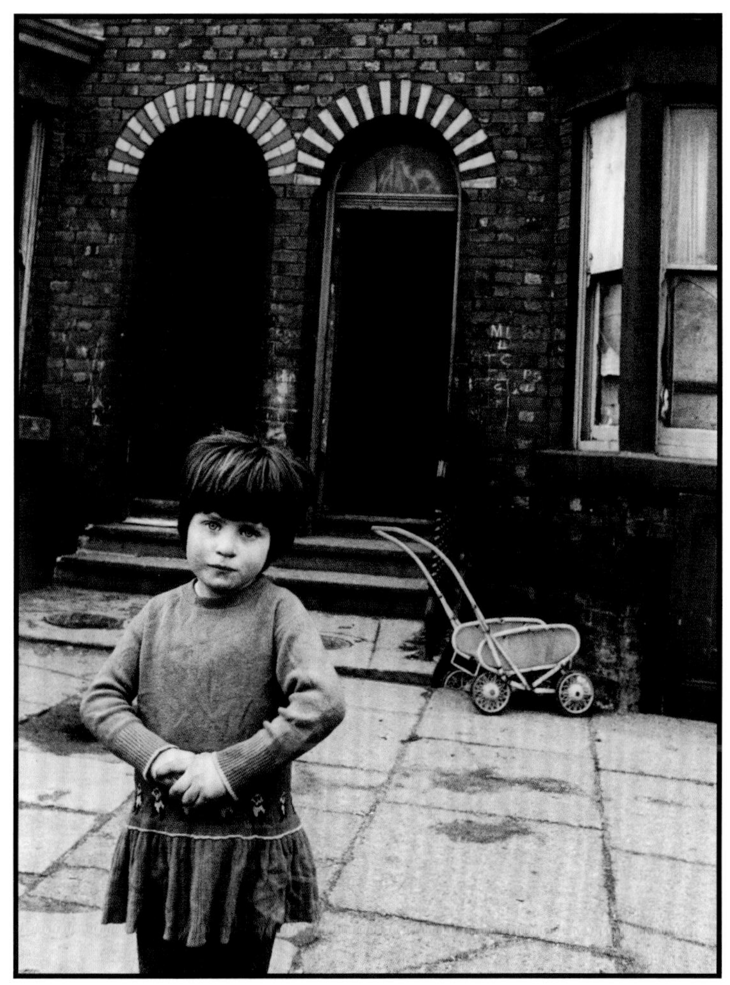

22

CHILDREN UNDER STRESS,
THE SUNDAY TIMES MAGAZINE
1970

34

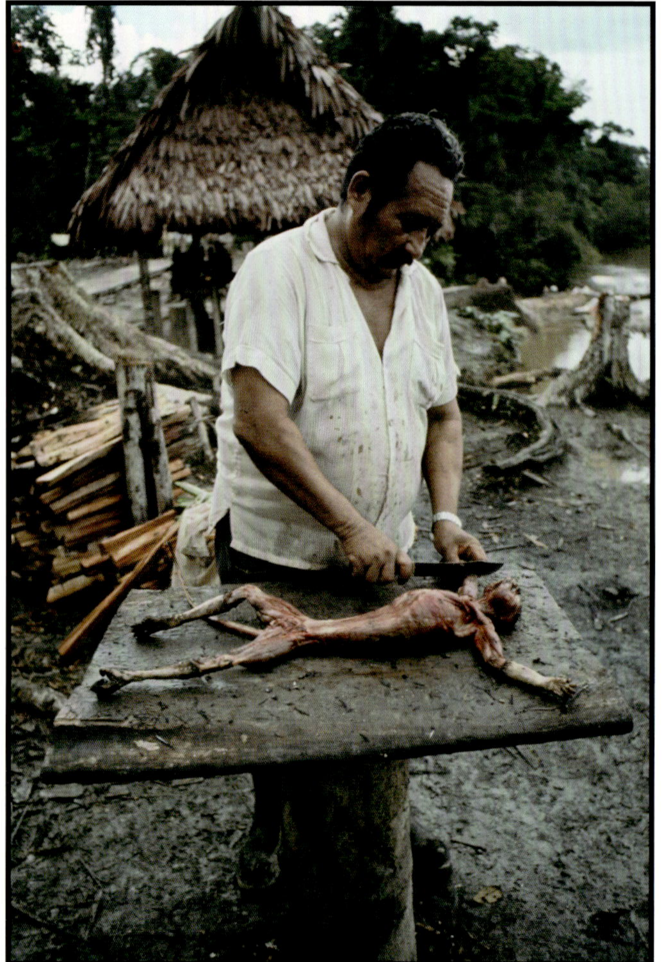

23
—

MONKEY SKINNING, PERU

1972

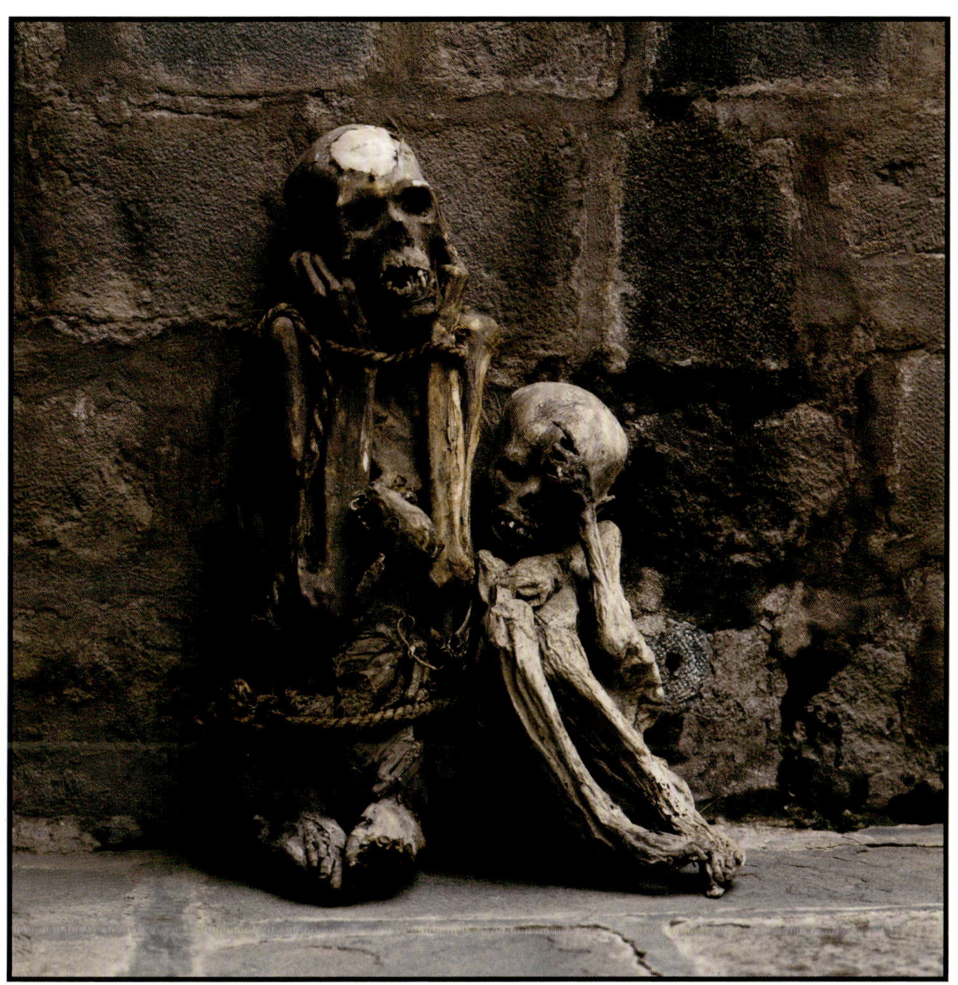

24

CATACOMBS, PERU

1972

36

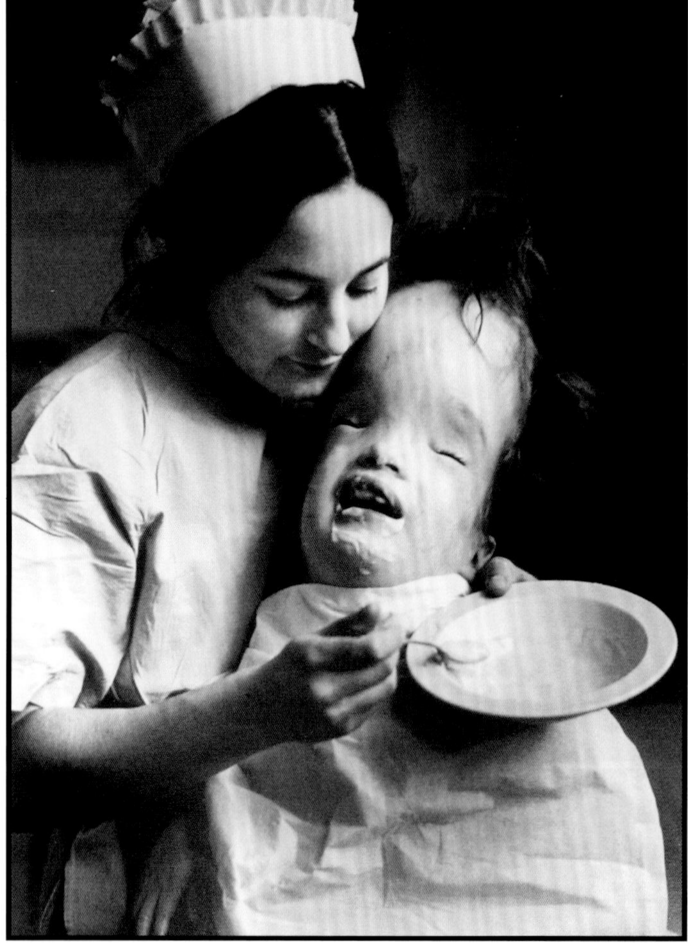

25

NURSE AND HYDROCEPHALIC CHILD
1975

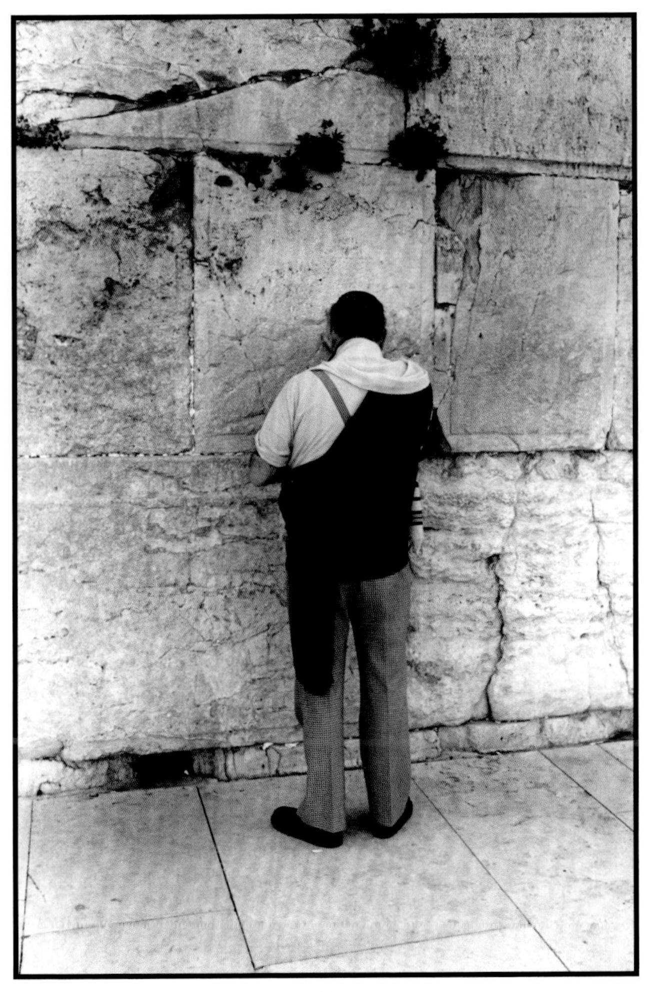

26

THE WAILING WALL, JERUSALEM
1985

38

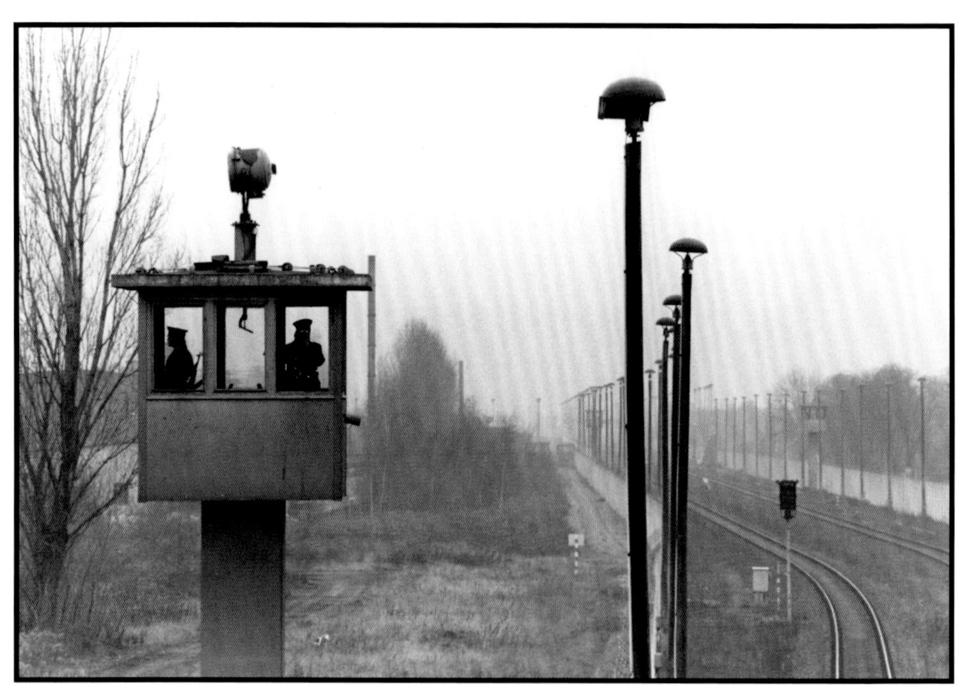

27
—

BERLIN WALL
1986

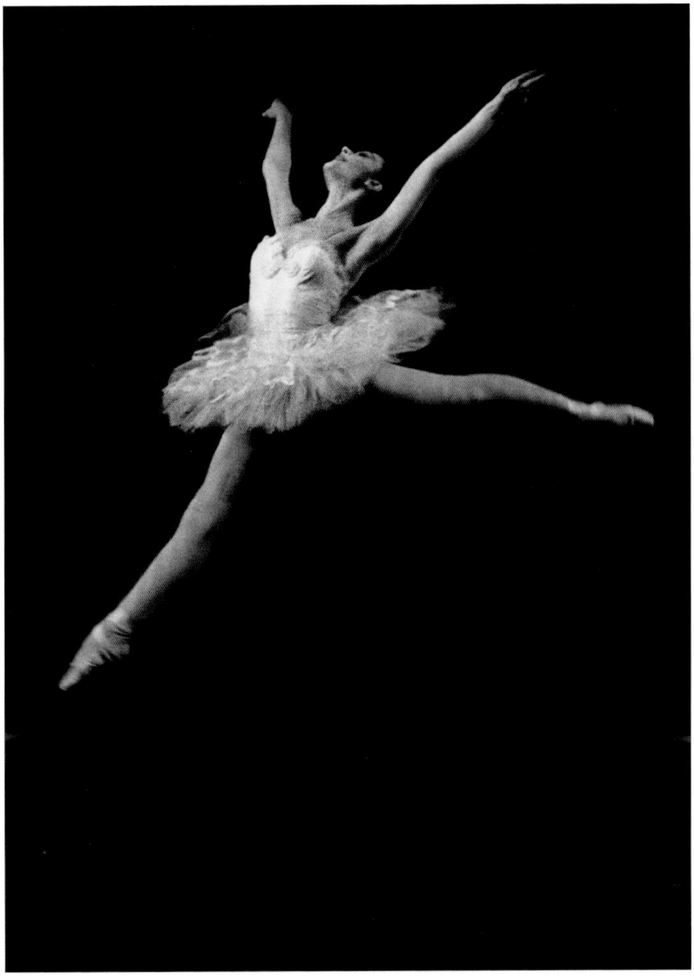

28
—

SVETLANA BERIOSOVA IN JOHN CRANKO'S *PRINCE OF THE PAGODAS*,
COVENT GARDEN, LONDON
1956

40

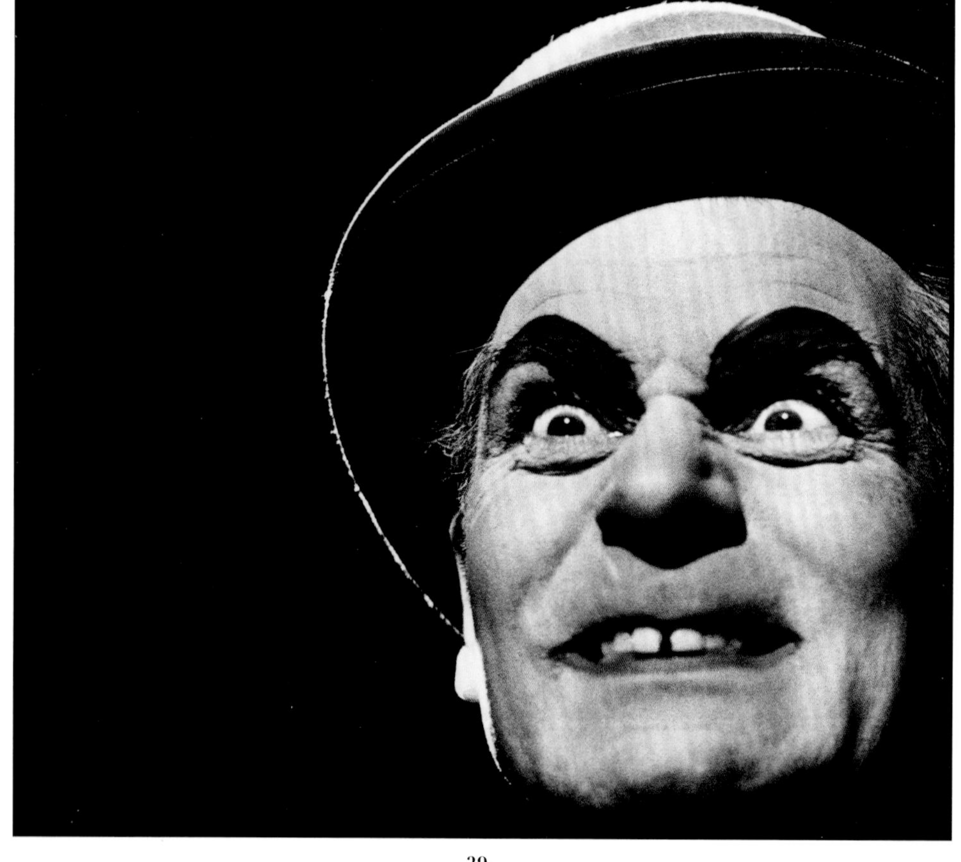

29

LAURENCE OLIVIER AS ARCHIE RICE IN *THE ENTERTAINER*,
ROYAL COURT THEATRE, LONDON
1957

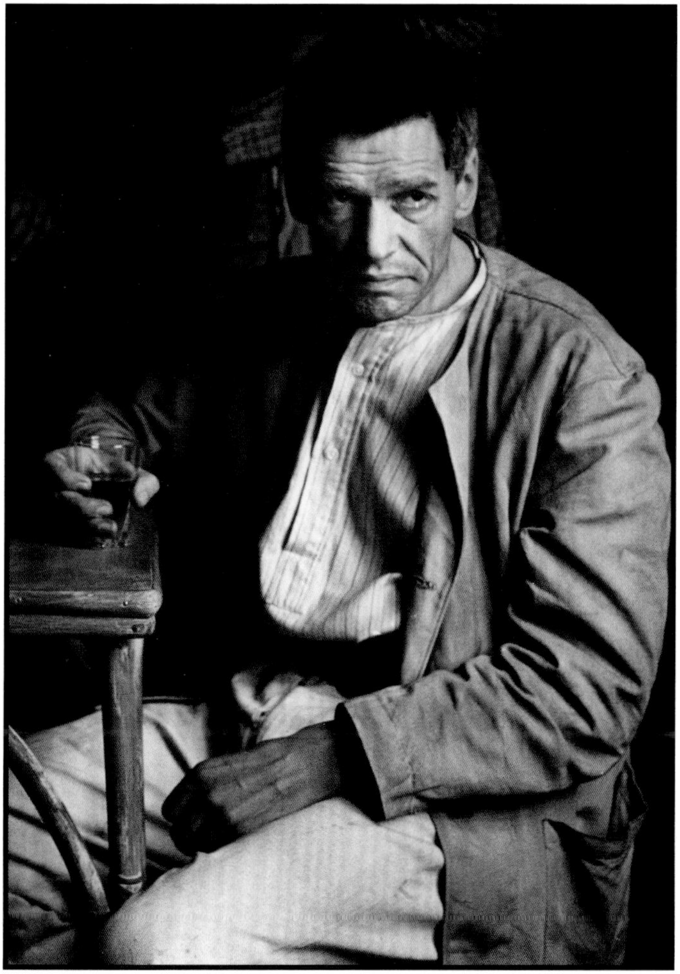

30

PAUL SCOFIELD IN *THE POWER AND THE GLORY*,
ROYAL COURT THEATRE, LONDON
1957

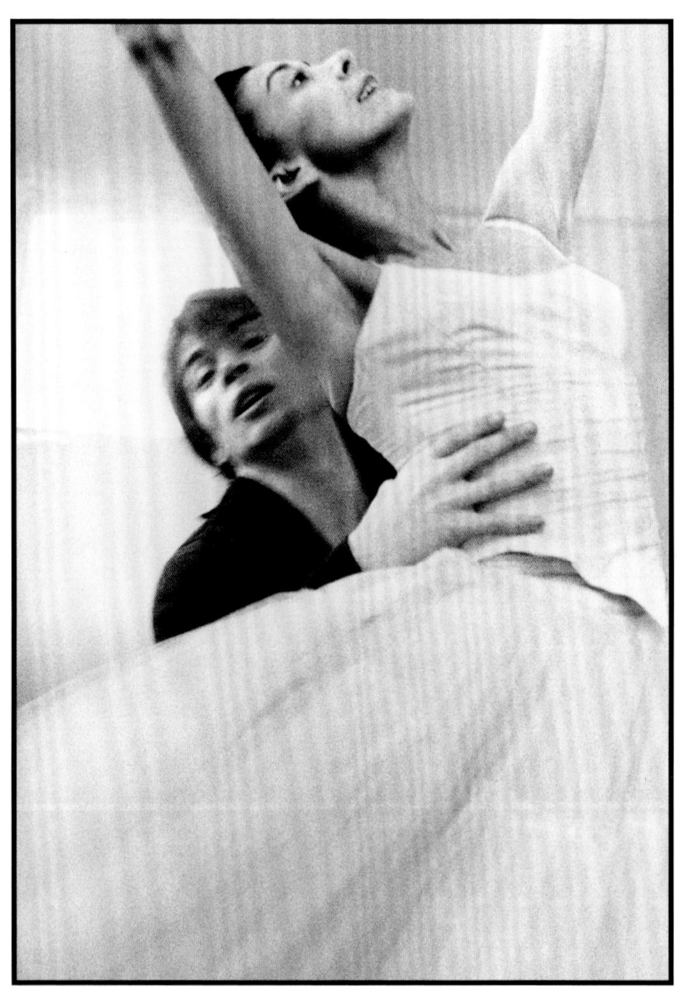

42

31

FONTEYN & NUREYEV REHEARSING *MARGUERITE AND ARMAND*,
ROYAL BALLET SCHOOL, LONDON

1963

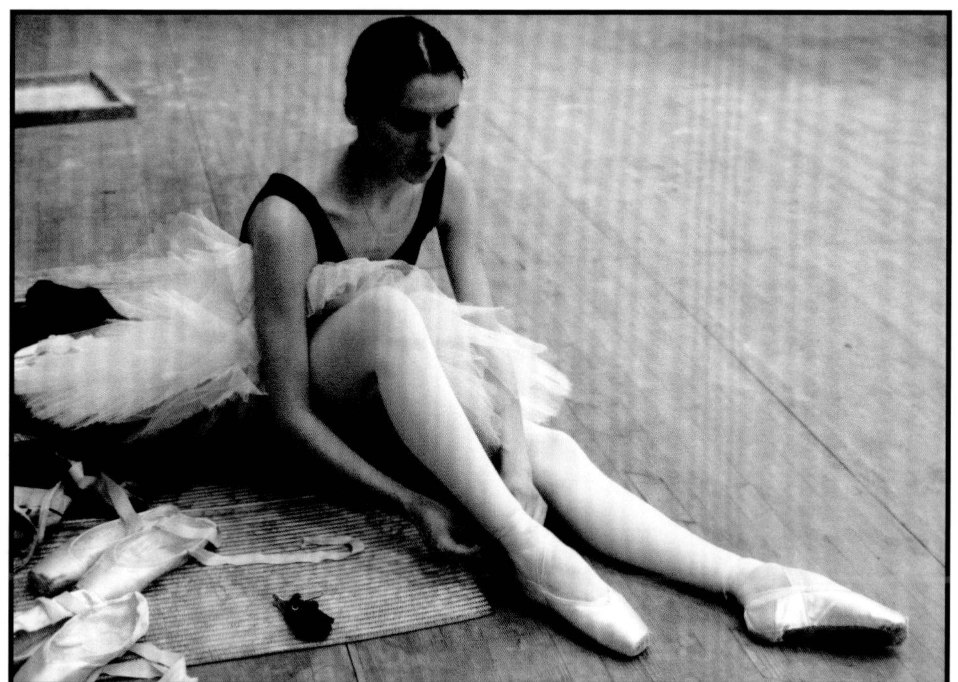

43

32
—
STUDENT AT THE VAGANOVA SCHOOL, ST PETERSBURG

2002

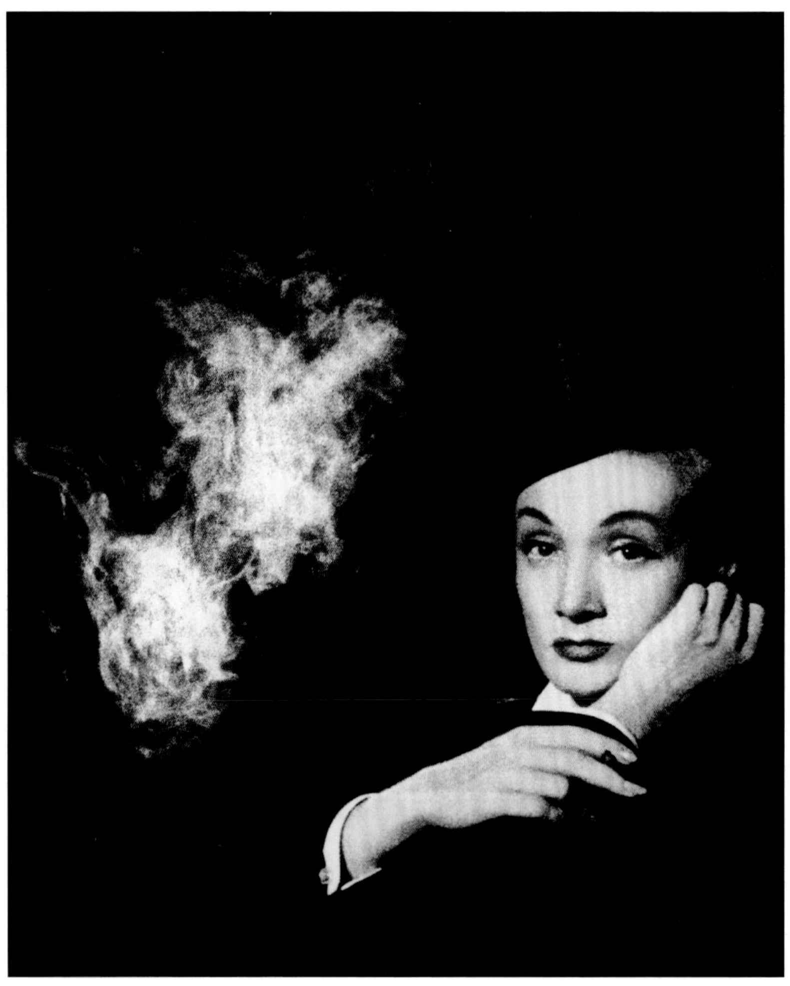

33
—

MARLENE DIETRICH, THE CAFÉ DE PARIS, LONDON,
1955

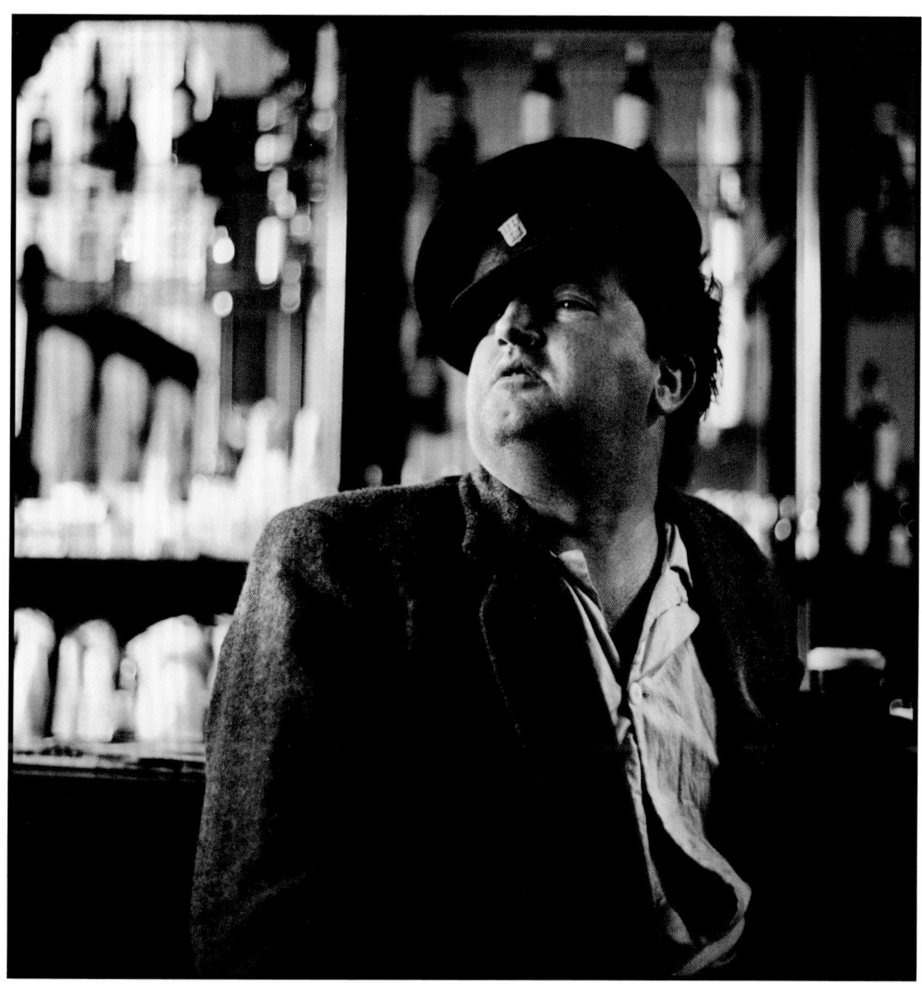

45

34

BRENDAN BEHAN, DUBLIN
1957

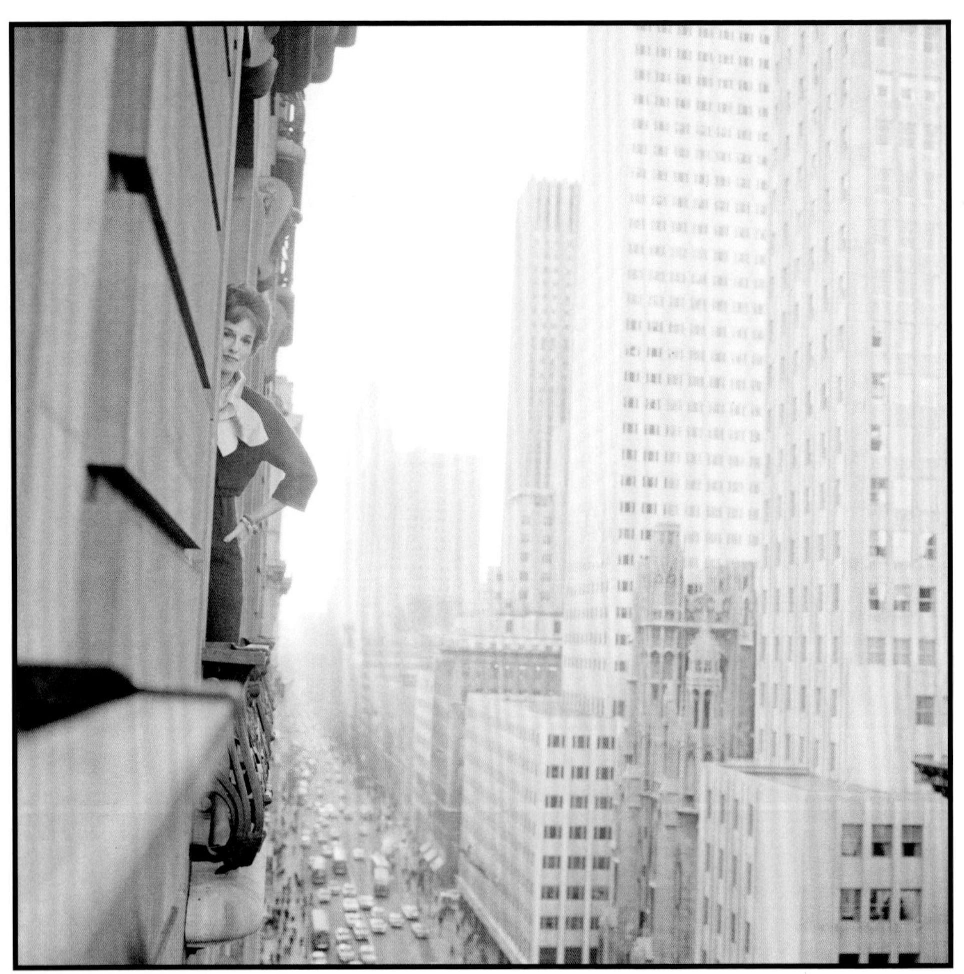

35

BABE PALEY, NEW YORK CITY

1958

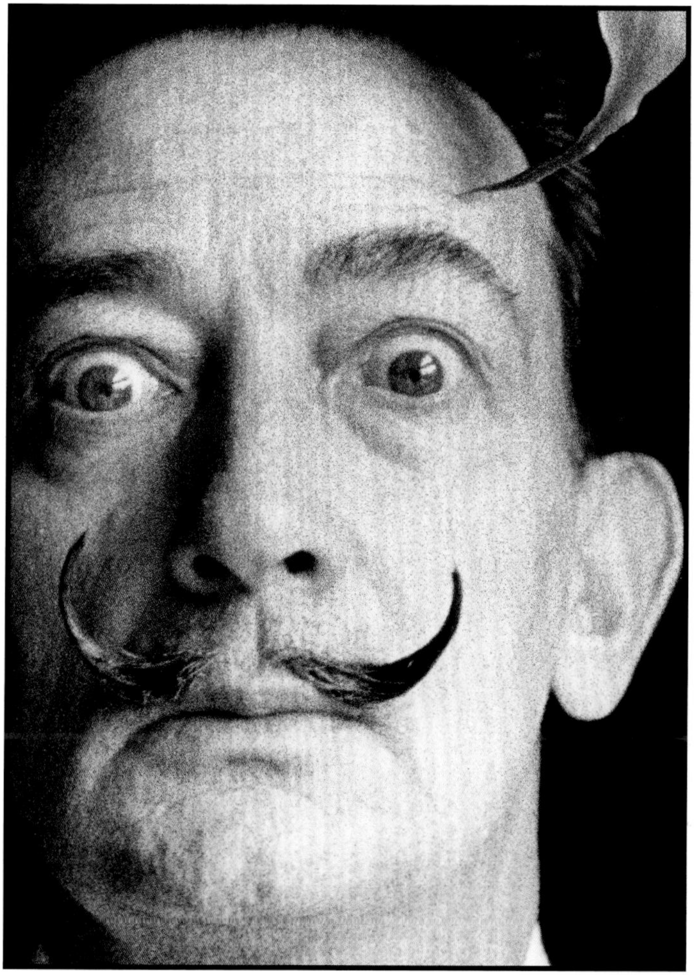

36

SALVADOR DALI

1958

48

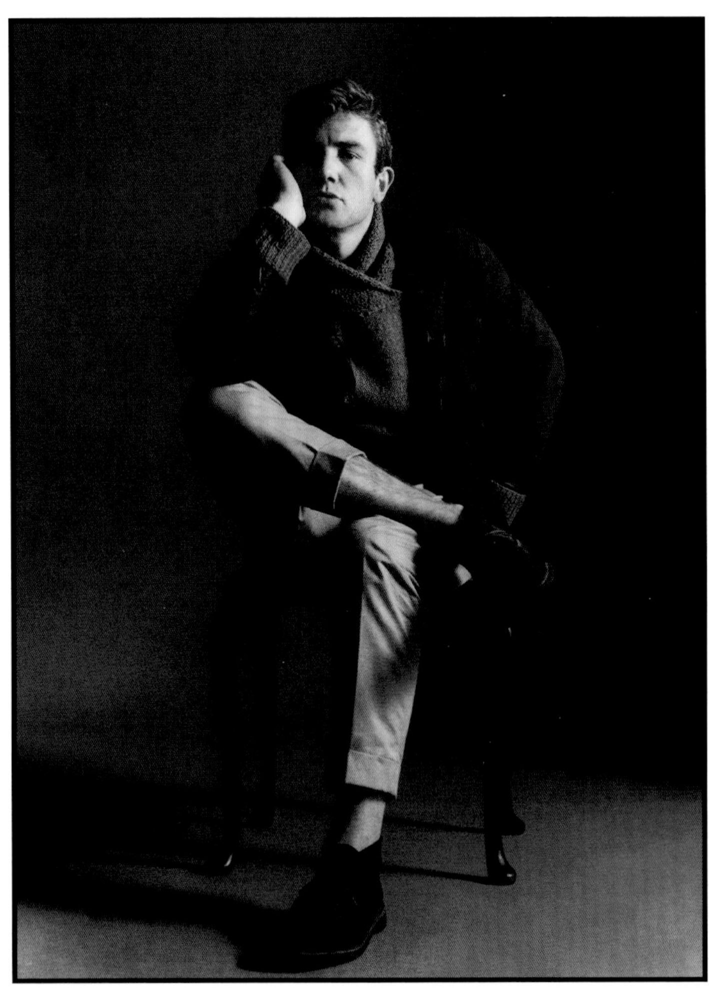

37

ALBERT FINNEY PHOTOGRAPHED FOR *QUEEN* MAGAZINE
1960

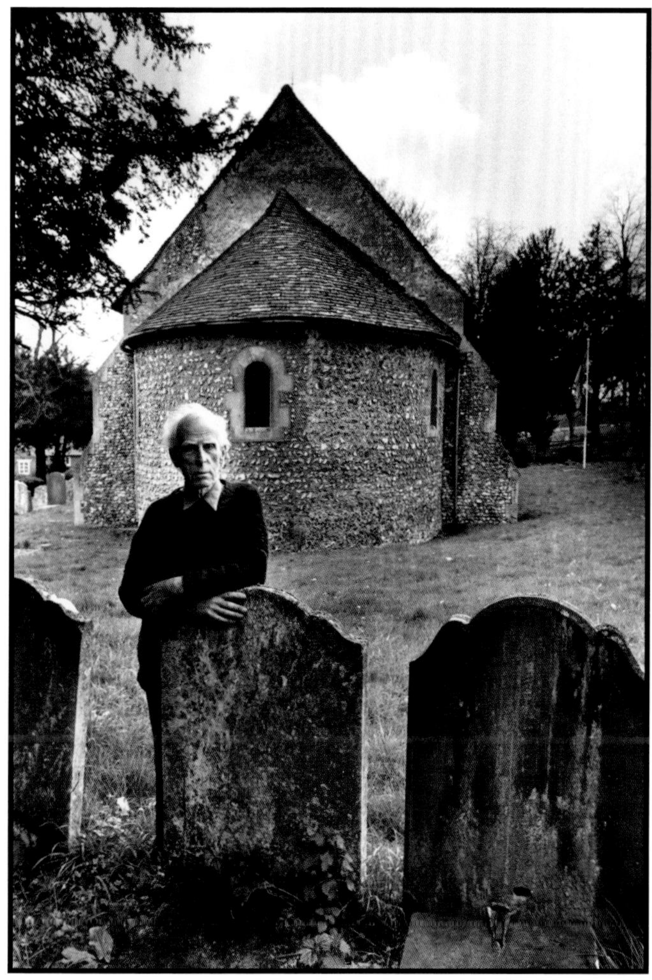

38

JOHN PIPER, HENLEY
1963

50

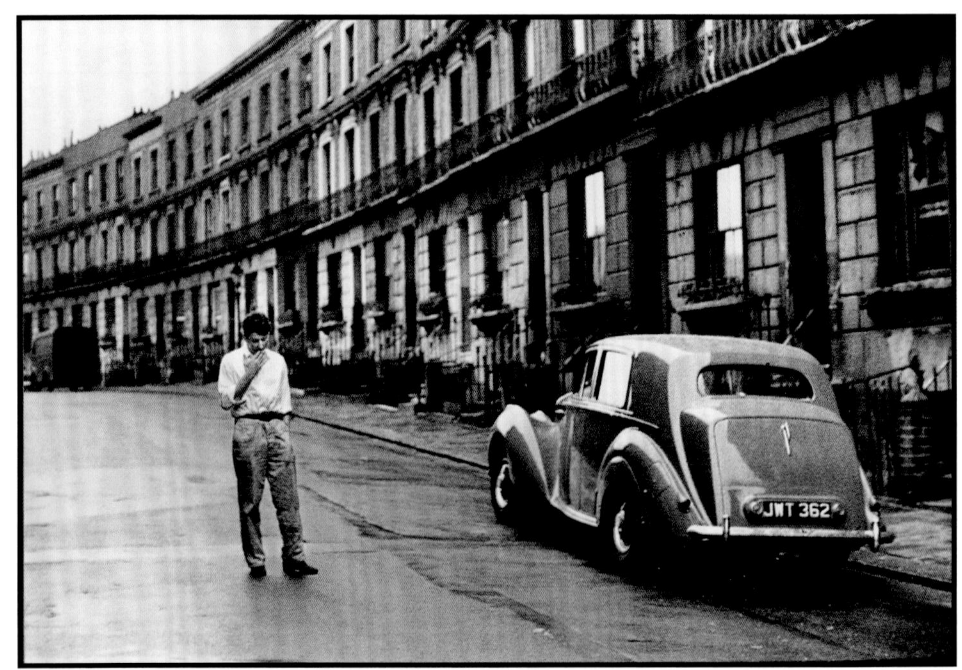

39

LUCIEN FREUD, PADDINGTON, LONDON
1963

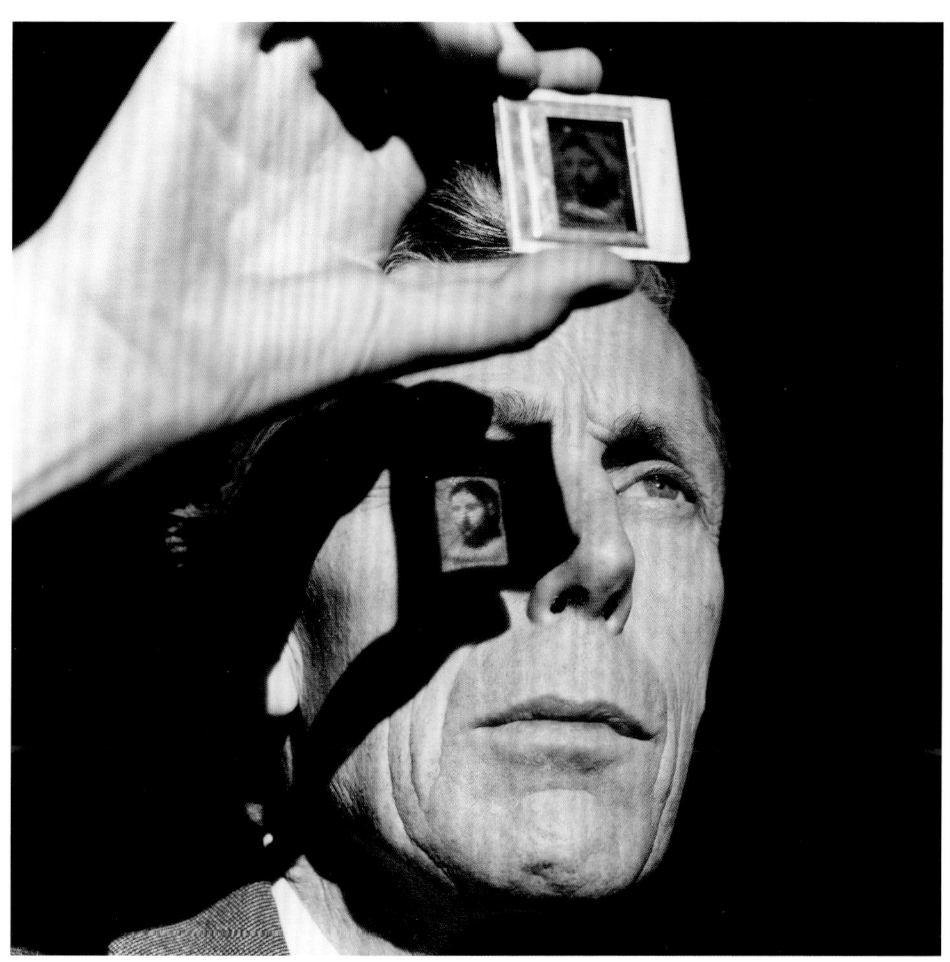

40

ANTHONY BLUNT, LONDON
1963

52

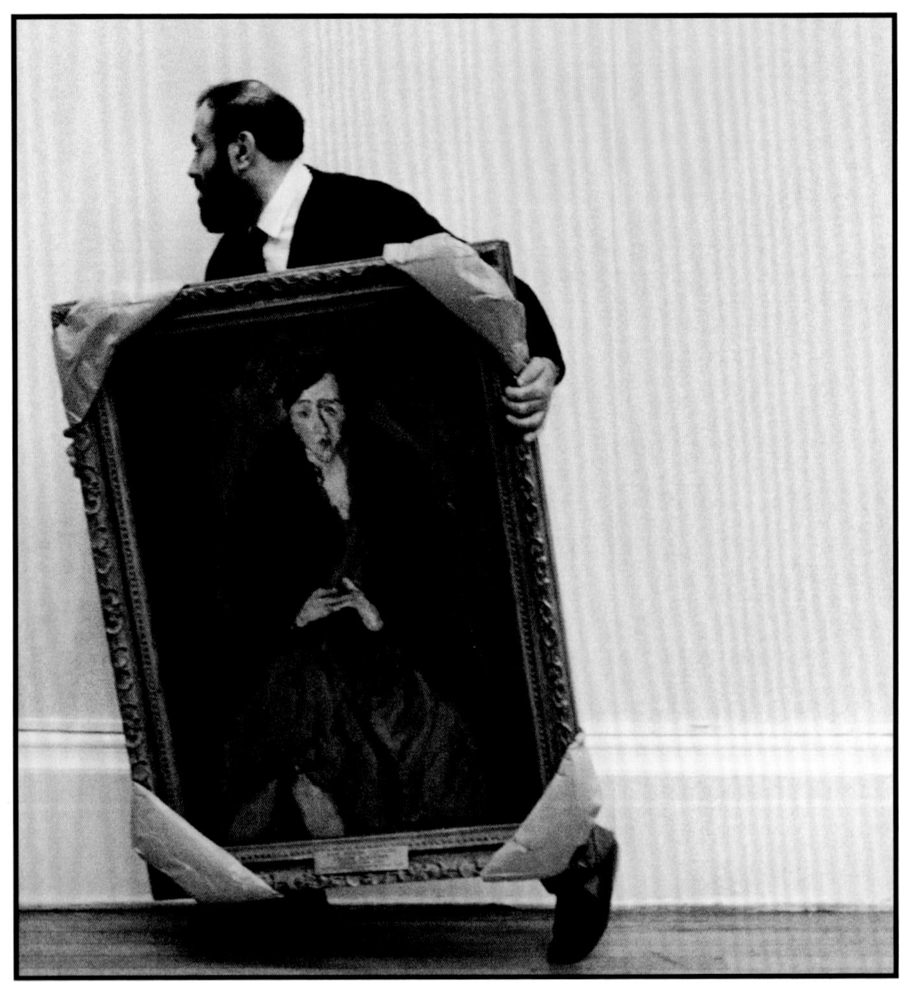

41

DAVID SYLVESTER, TATE GALLERY, LONDON
1963

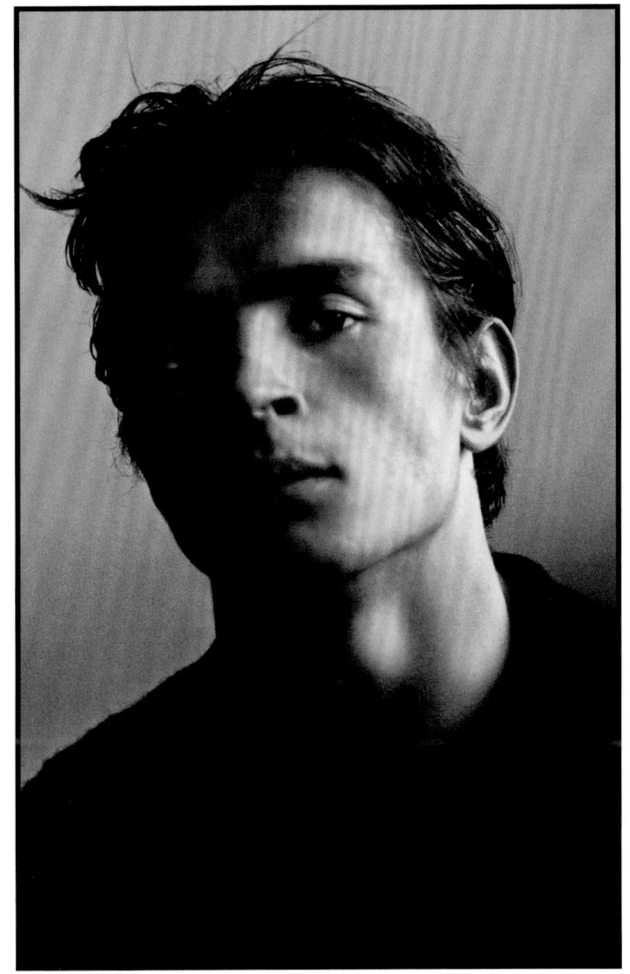

42
—

RUDOLPH NUREYEV, ROYAL BALLET SCHOOL, LONDON
1963

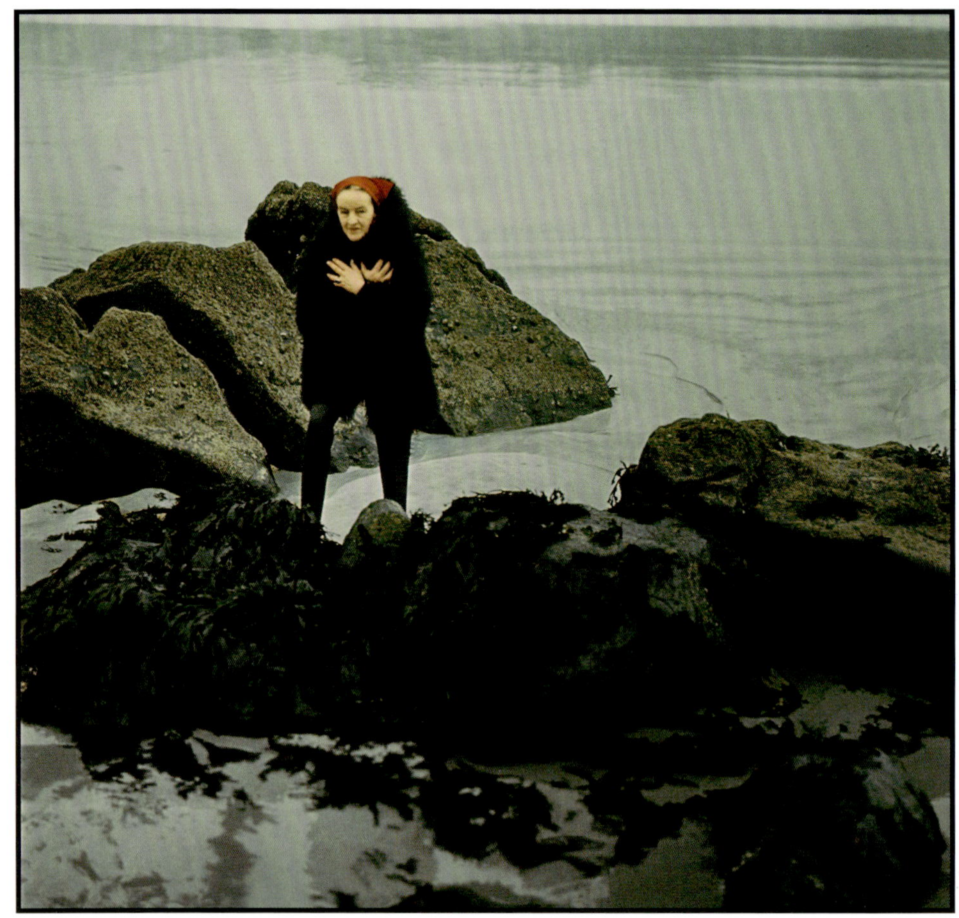

43
—

BARBARA HEPWORTH, ST IVES
1964

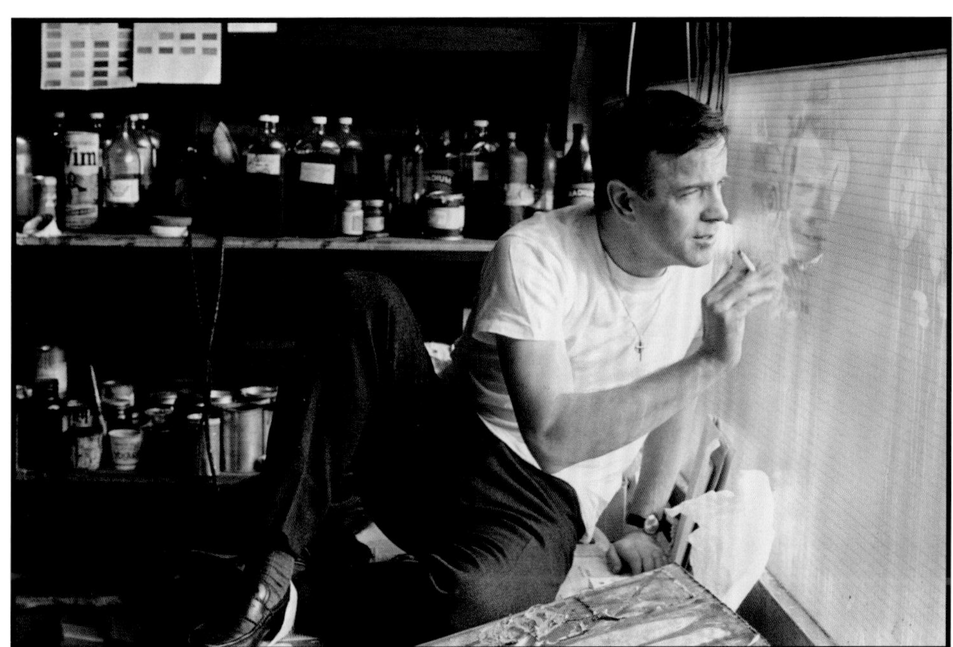

44

FRANCO ZEFFIRELLI, LONDON
1965

56

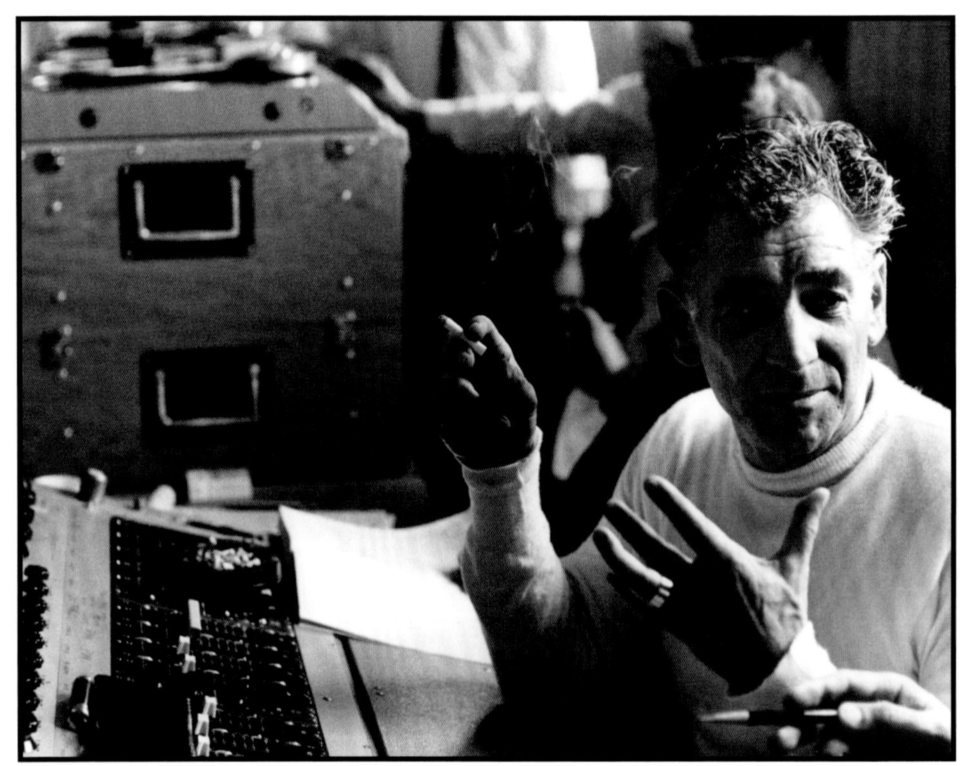

45
—

LEONARD BERNSTEIN
1966

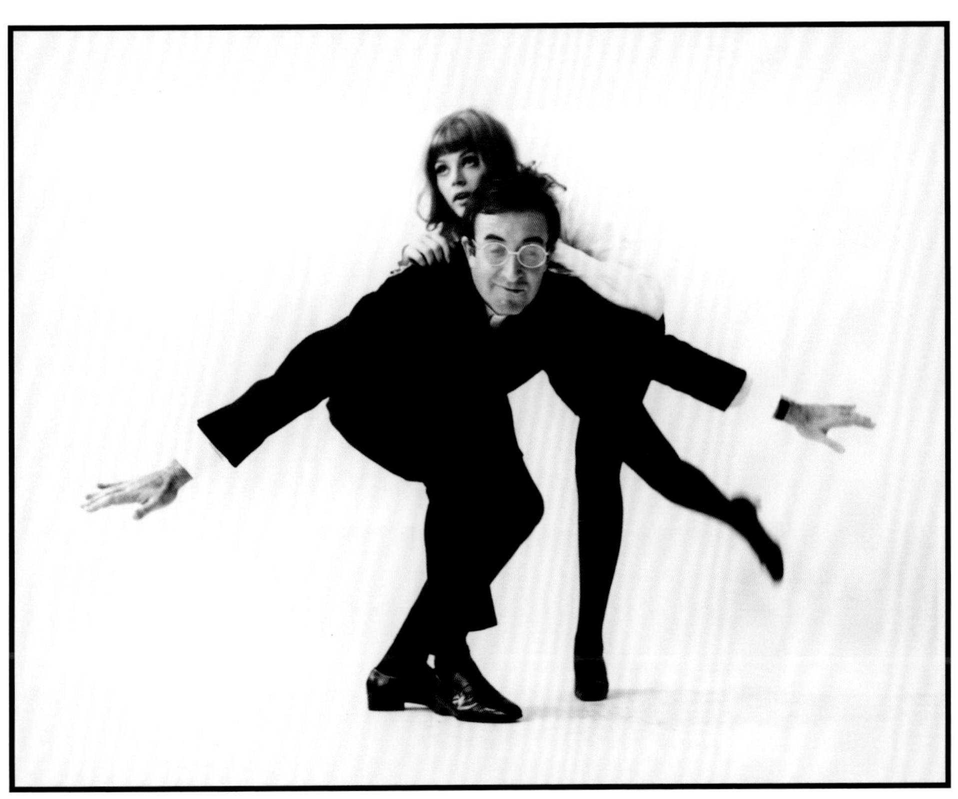

46

PETER SELLERS AND BRITT EKLAND
1967

58

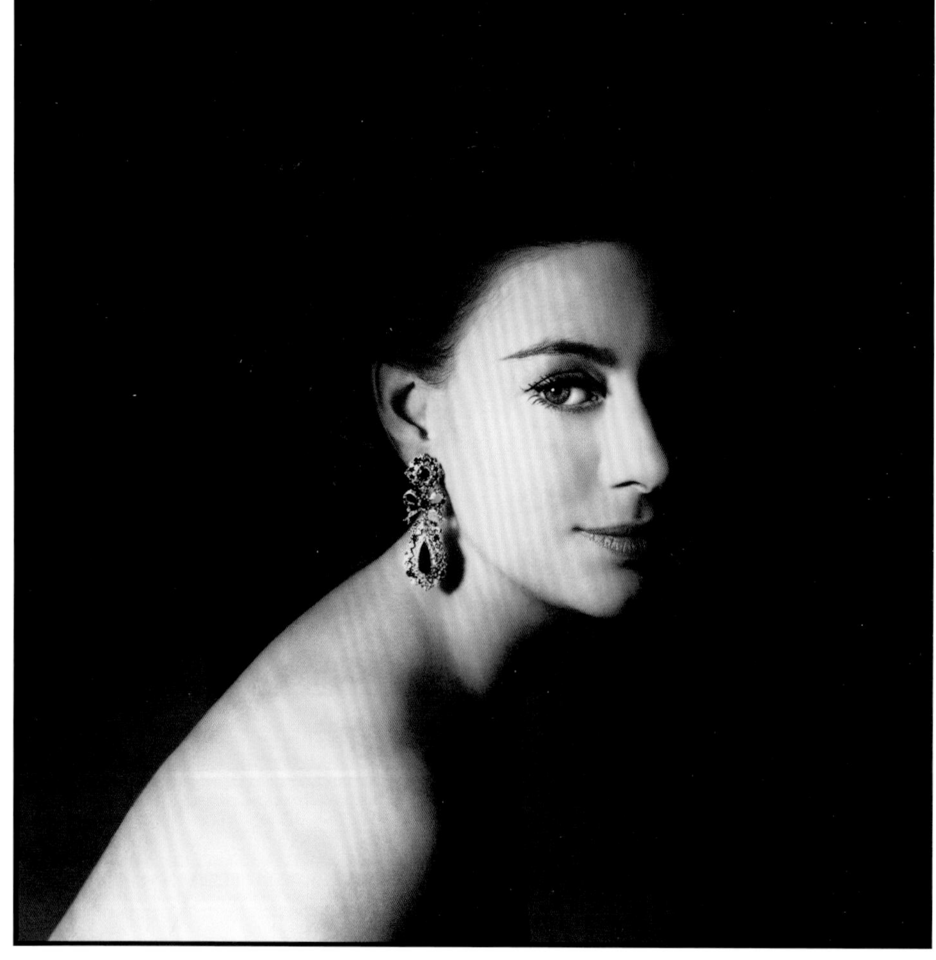

47

PRINCESS MARGARET, LONDON
1967

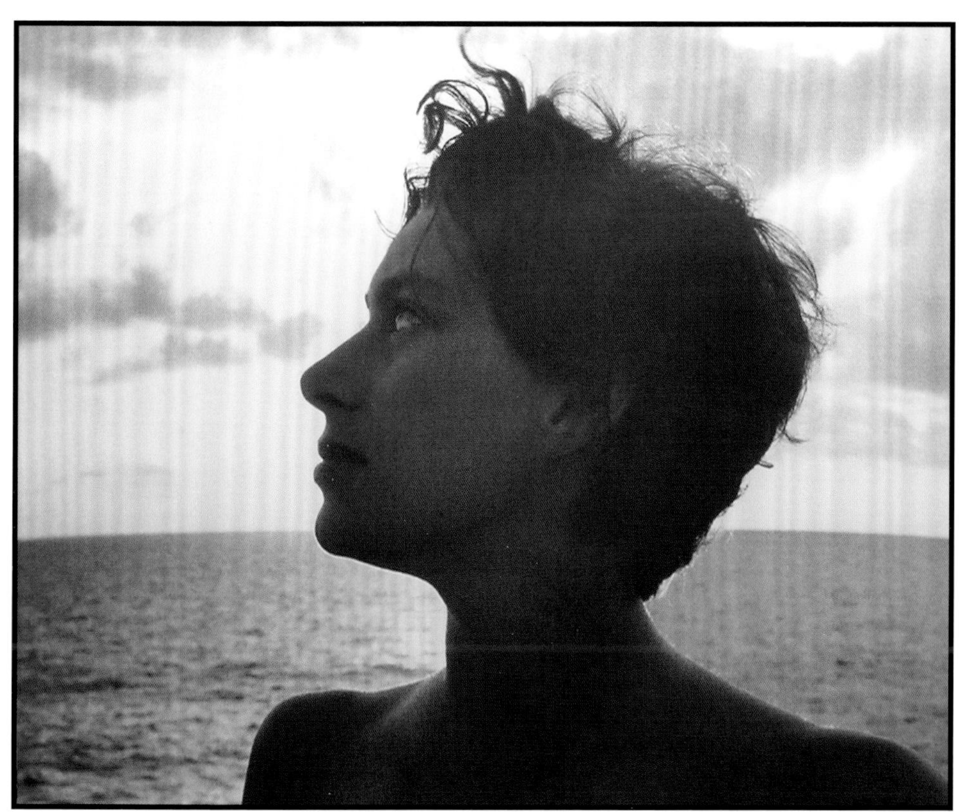

48
—

PRINCESS MARGARET, CARIBBEAN
1960s

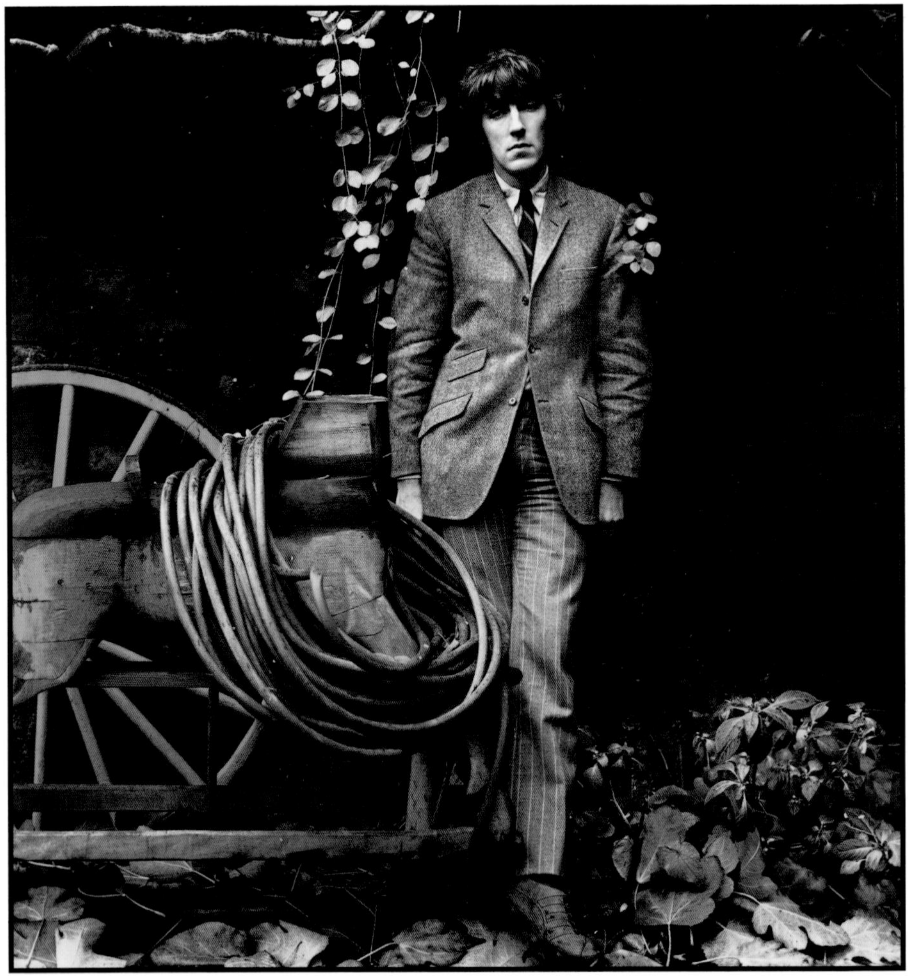

49
—
PETER COOK, CAMDEN TOWN, LONDON
1967

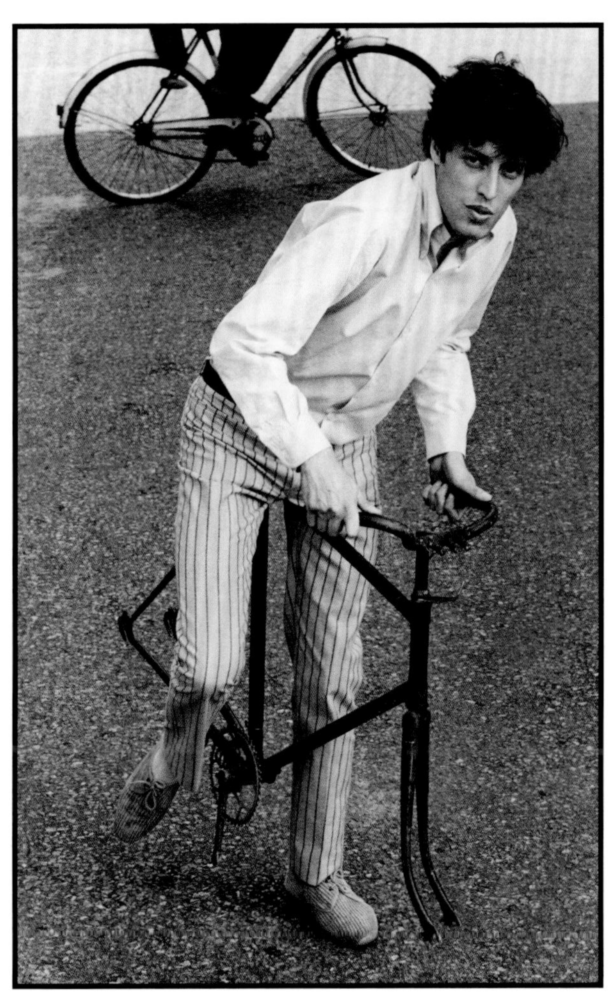

50
—

TOM STOPPARD, ROTHERHITHE, LONDON
1967

62

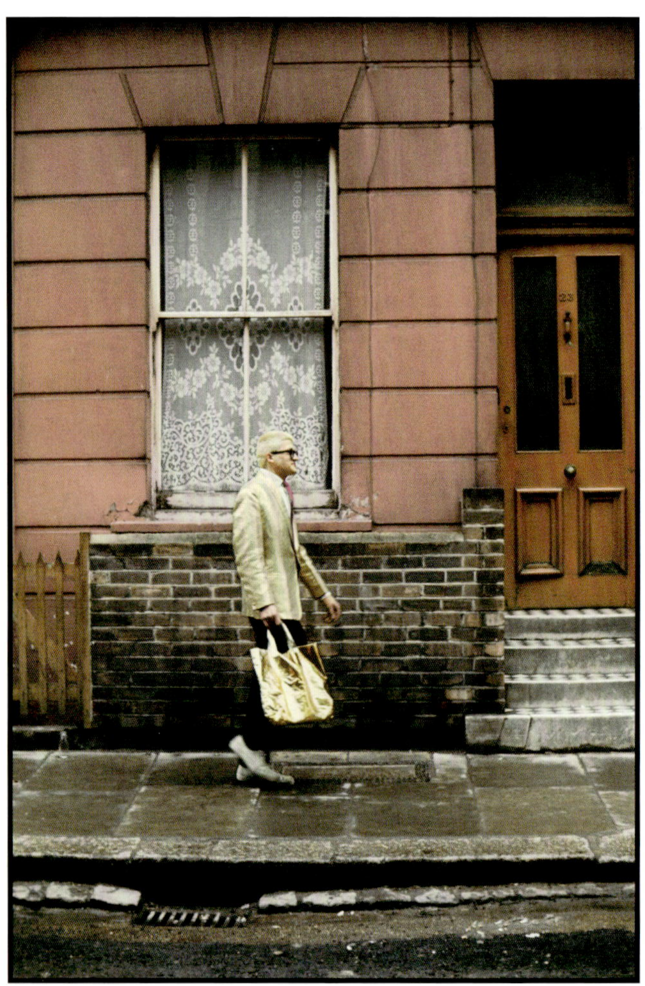

51

DAVID HOCKNEY, PADDINGTON, LONDON

1968

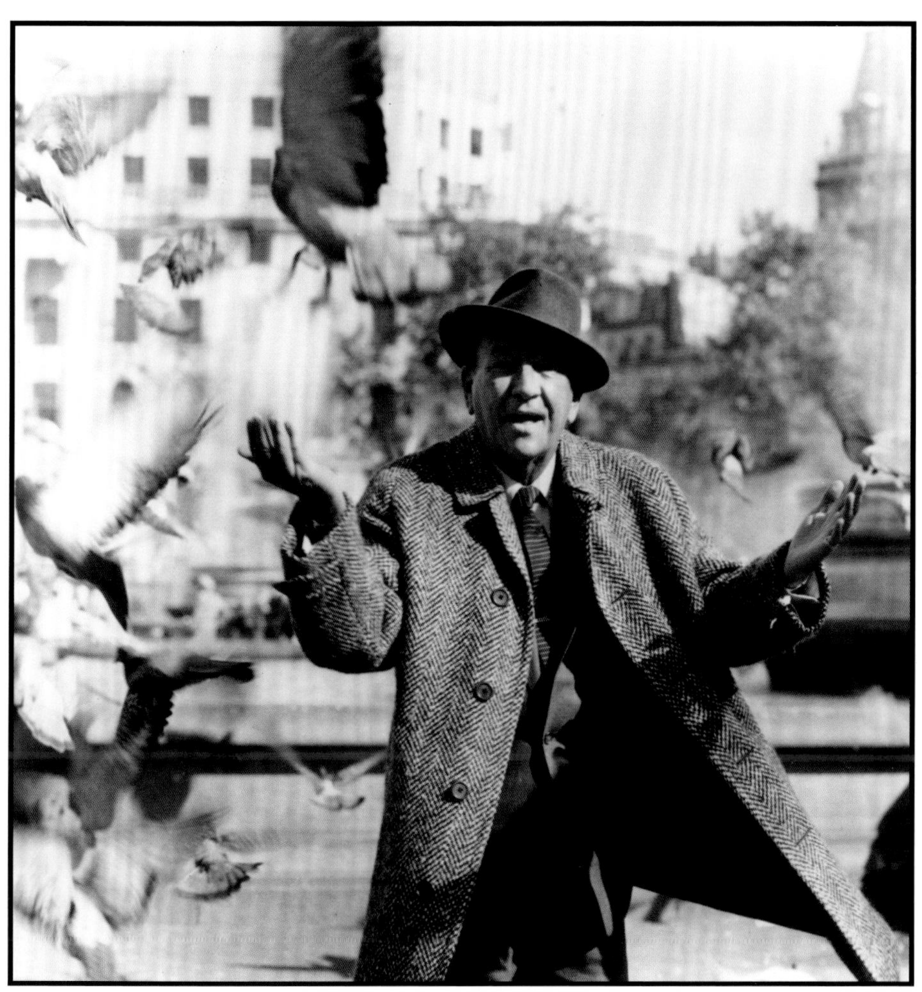

52

NOEL COWARD, TRAFALGAR SQUARE, LONDON

1970

64

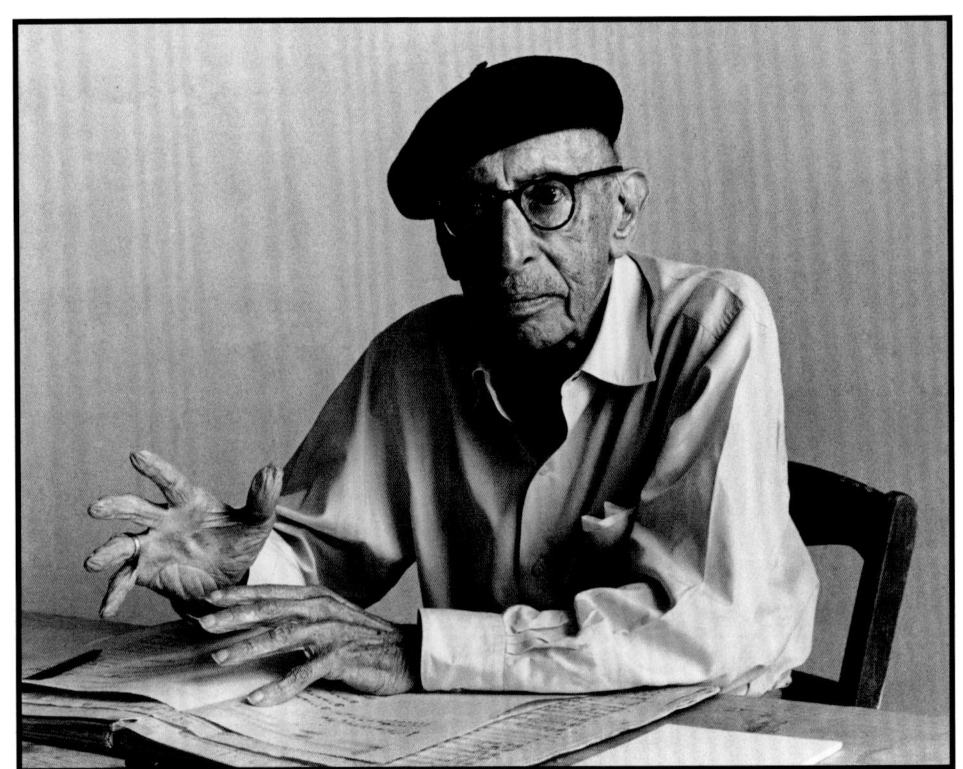

53
—

IGOR STRAVINSKY

1970

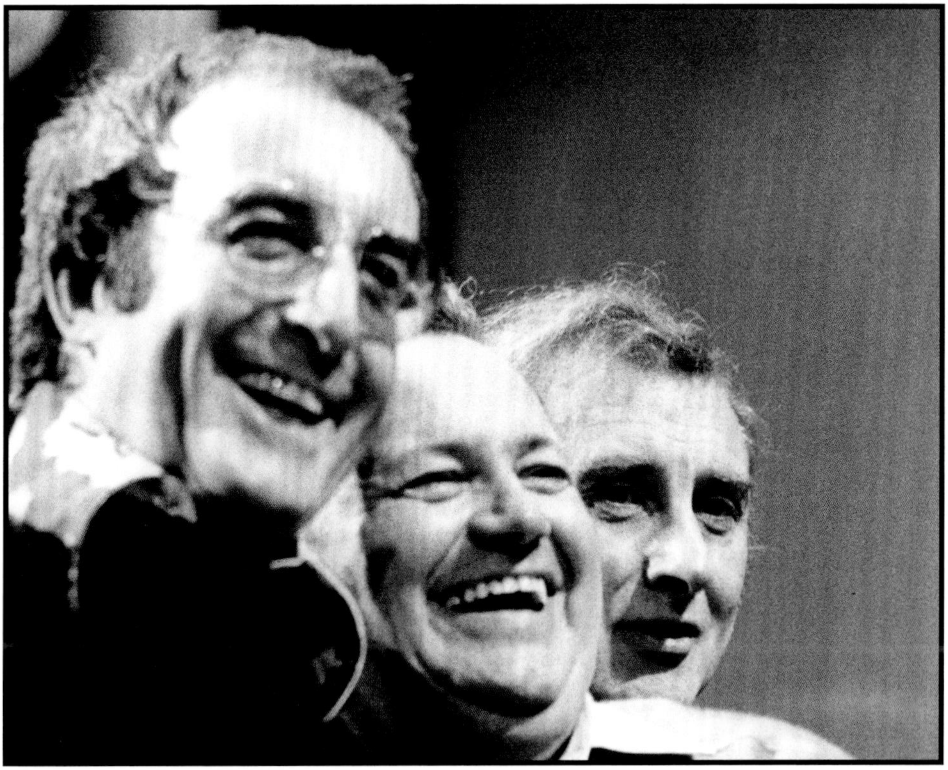

65

54

THE GOONS

1972

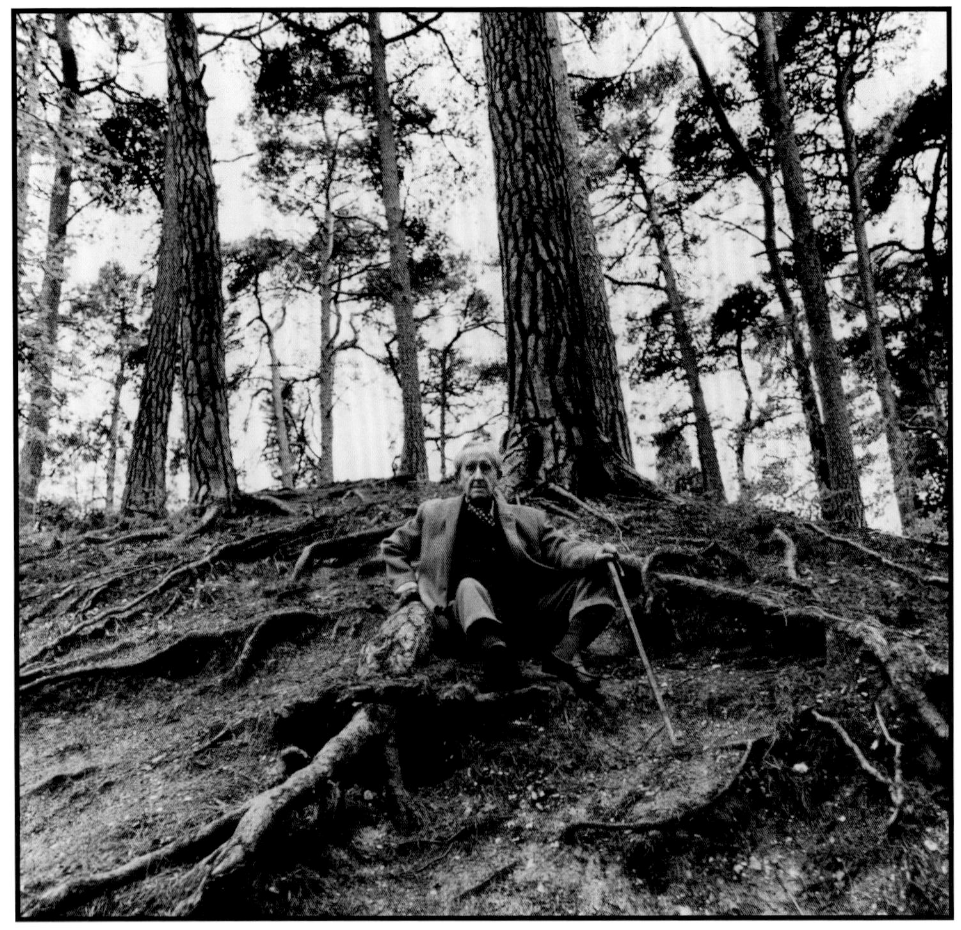

55

J.R.R. TOLKIEN, BOURNEMOUTH

1972

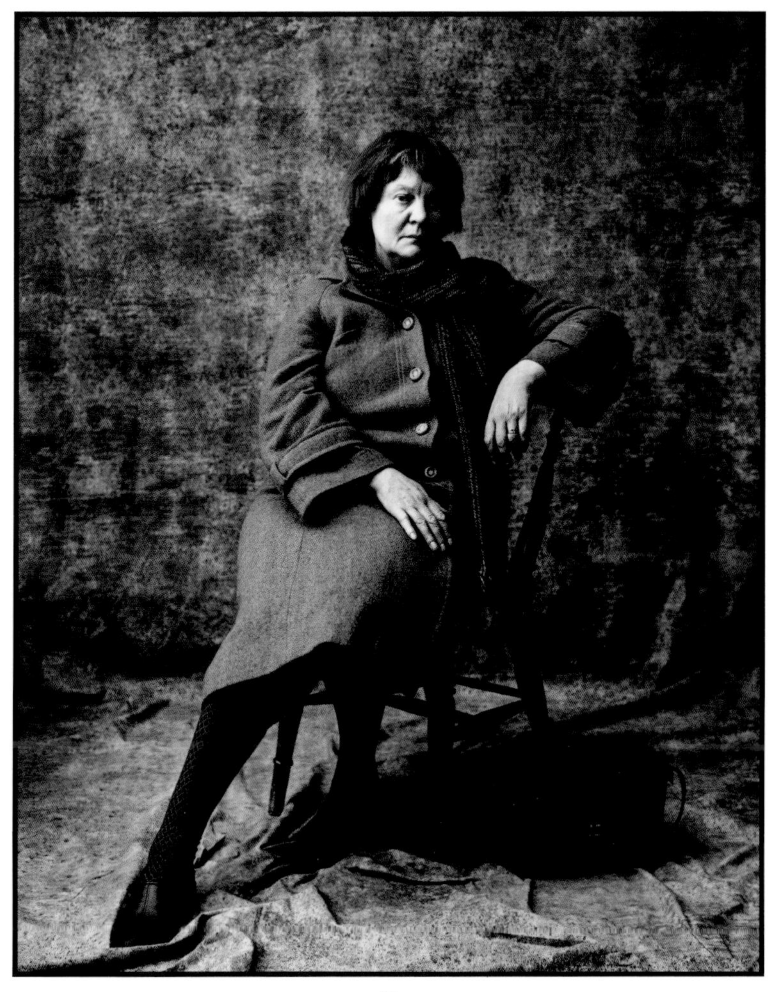

56
—

IRIS MURDOCH
1980

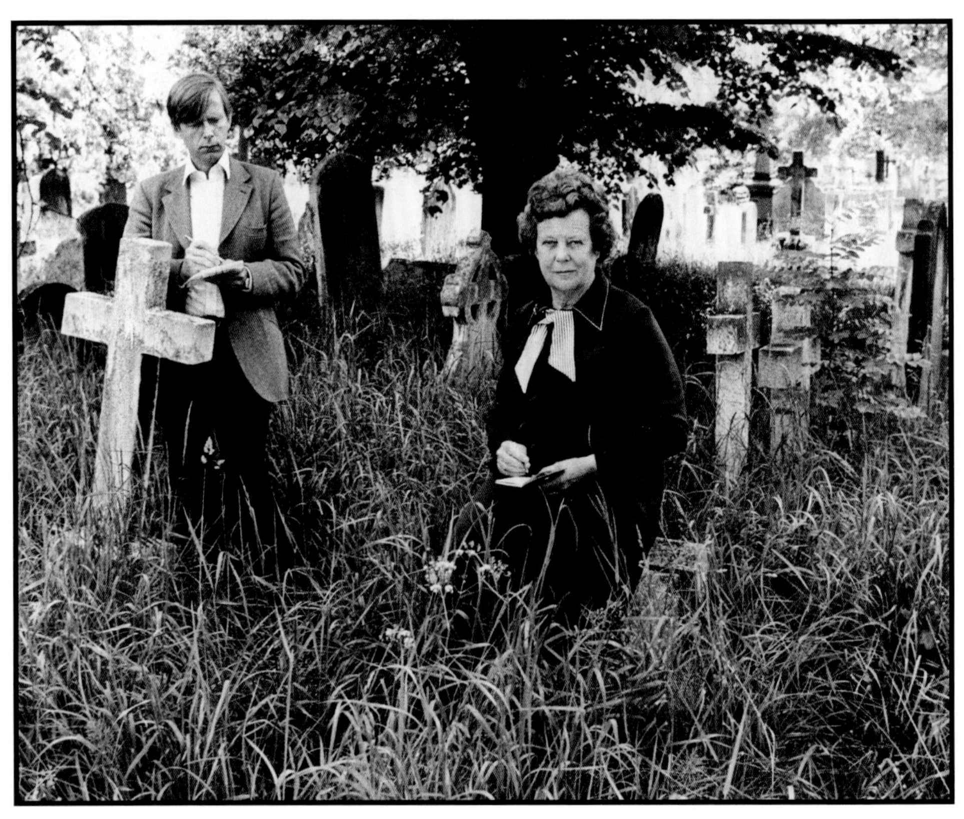

57

LADY MARY WILSON & JOHN WELLS, BROMPTON CEMETERY, LONDON
1980

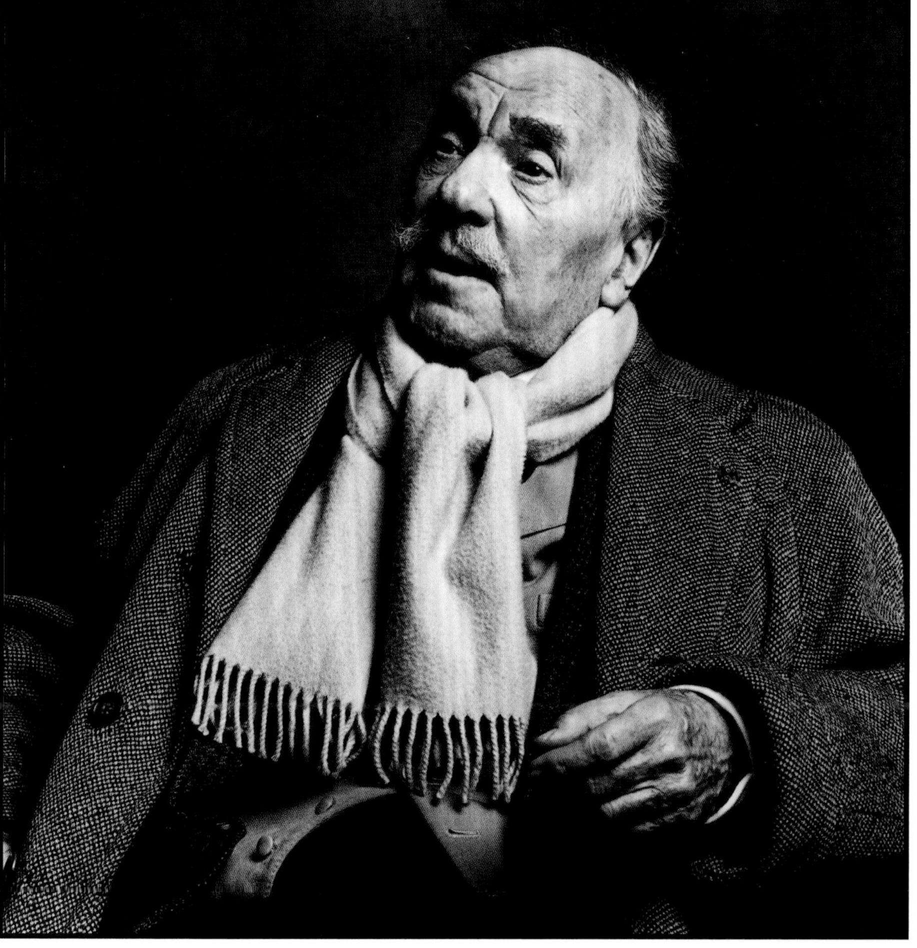

58

RALPH RICHARDSON
1981

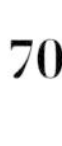

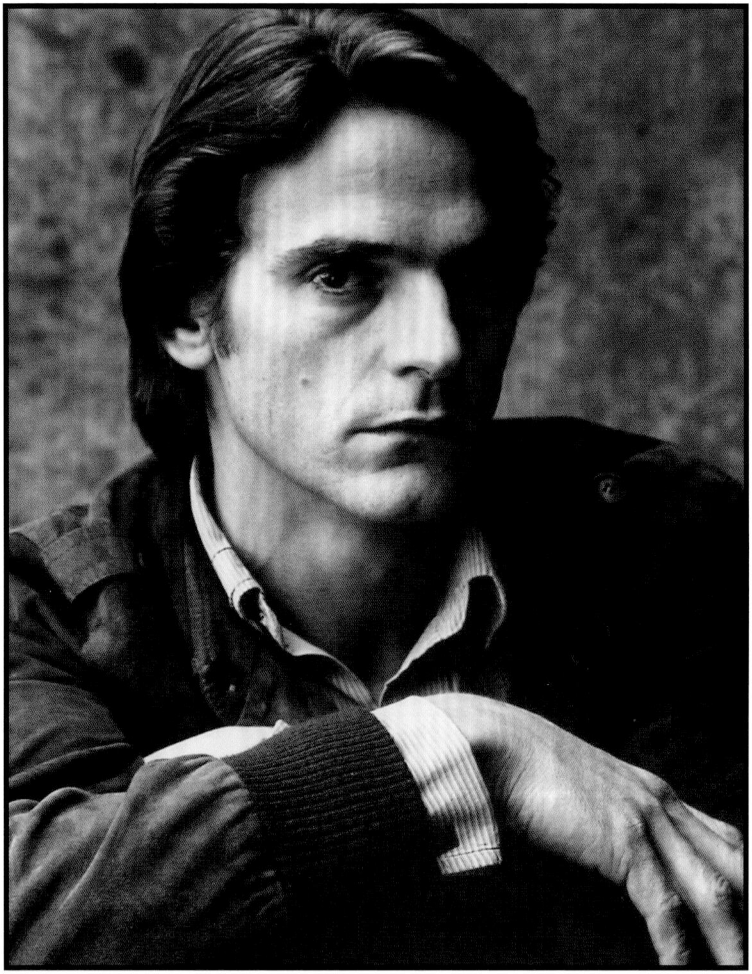

59

JEREMY IRONS

1981

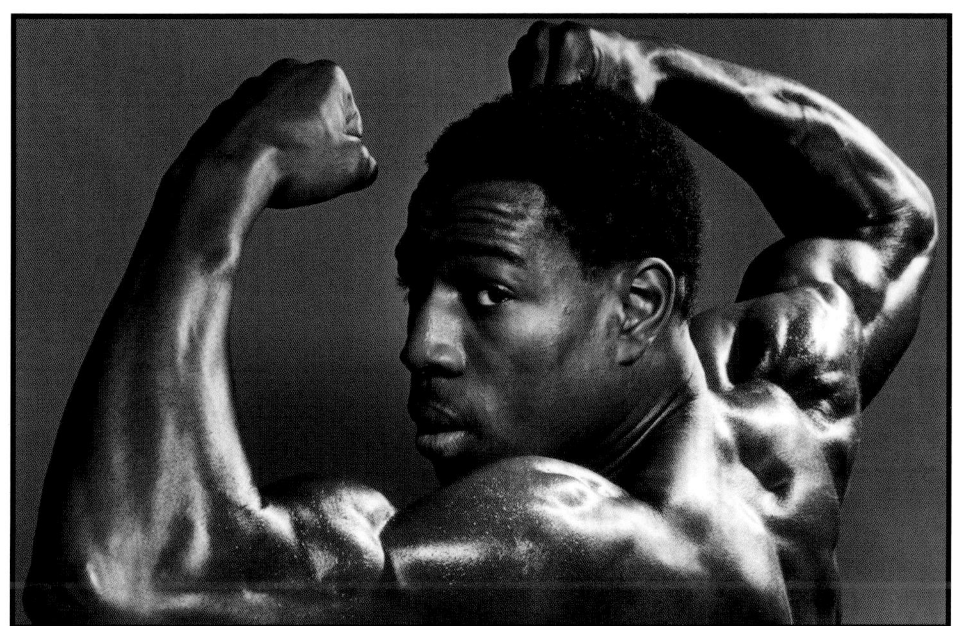

60

FRANK BRUNO

1983

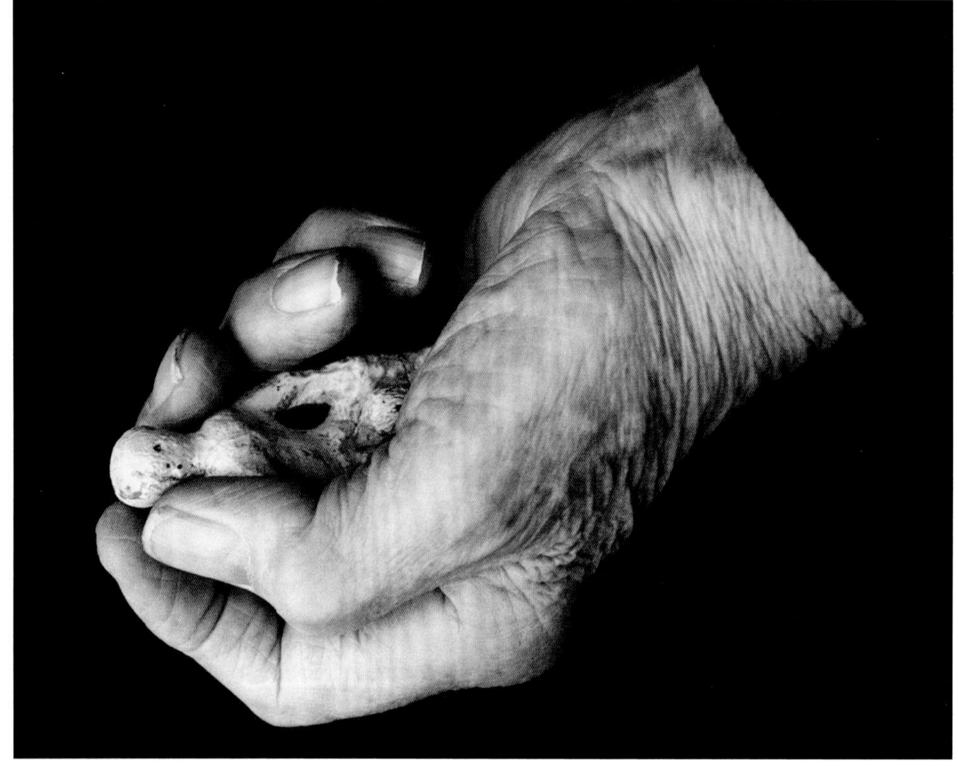

61

HENRY MOORE HOLDING A MAQUETTE OF *MOTHER AND CHILD*
1983

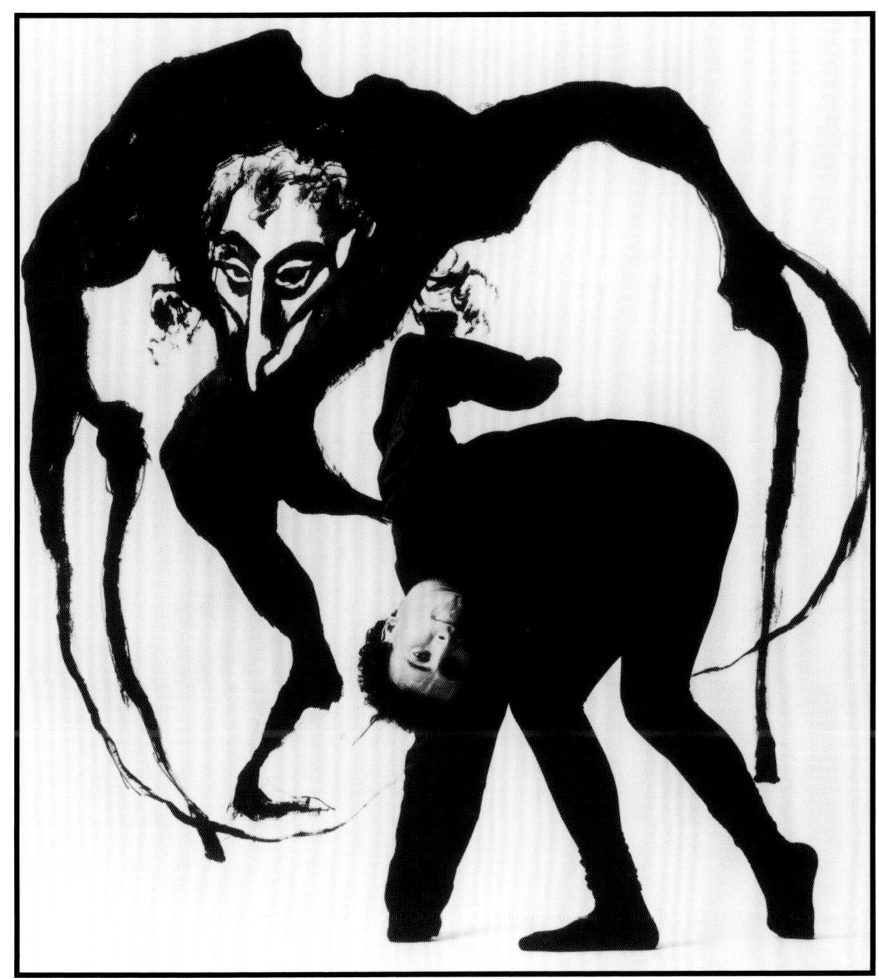

62

ANTHONY SHER AS RICHARD III

1985

74

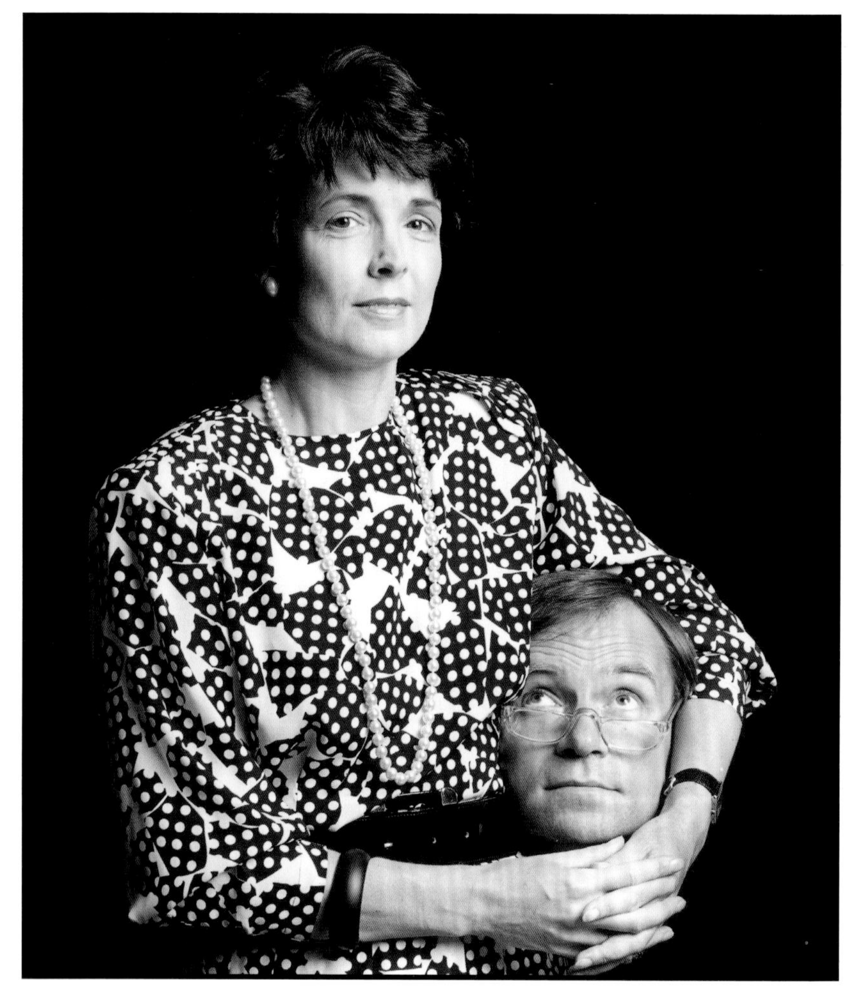

63

JEFFREY AND MARY ARCHER

1987

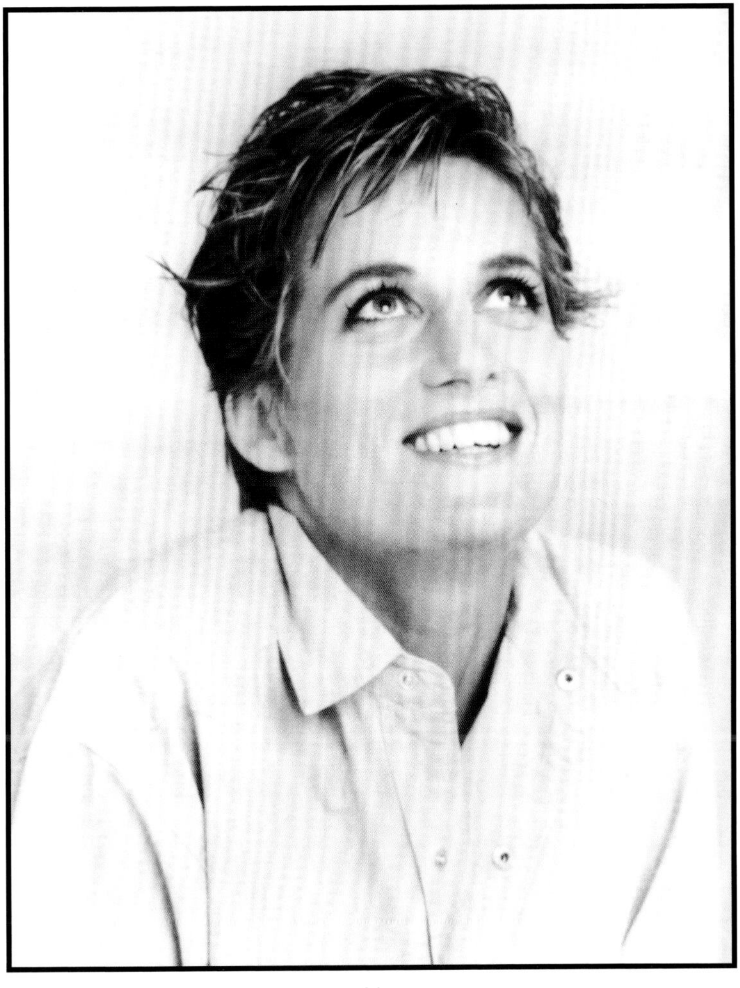

64

PRINCESS DIANA

1991

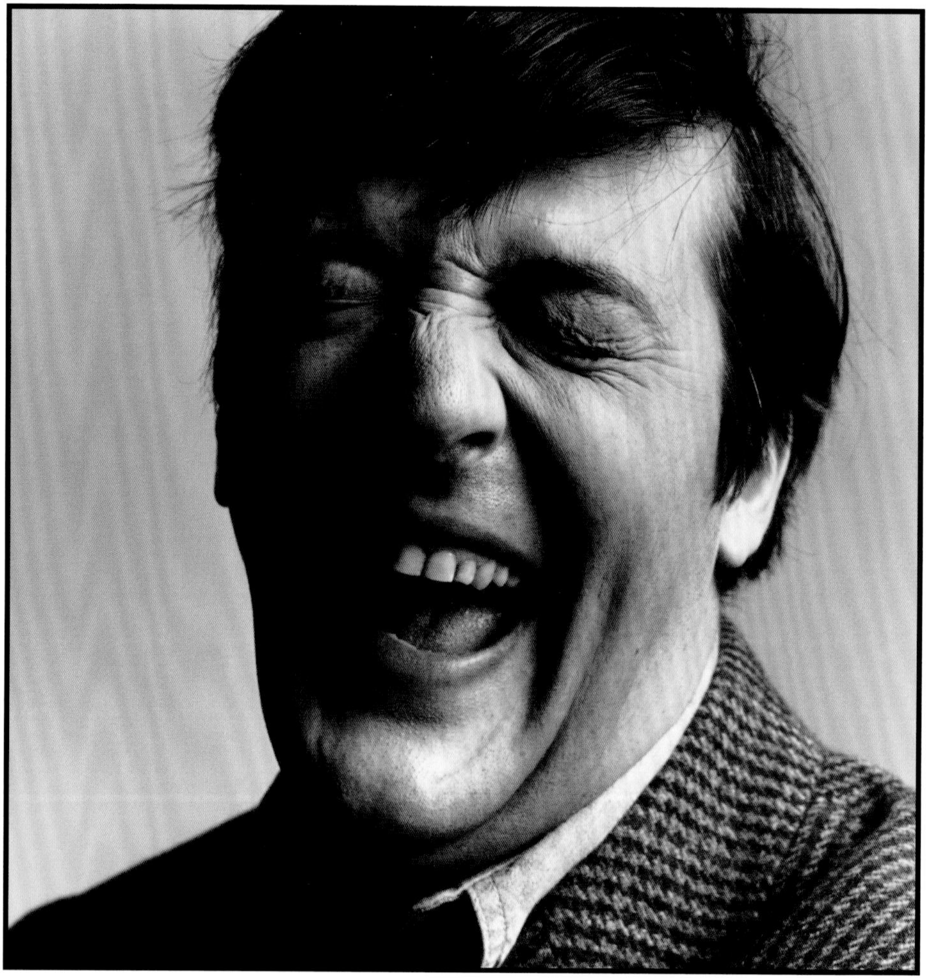

65

STEPHEN FRY

1994

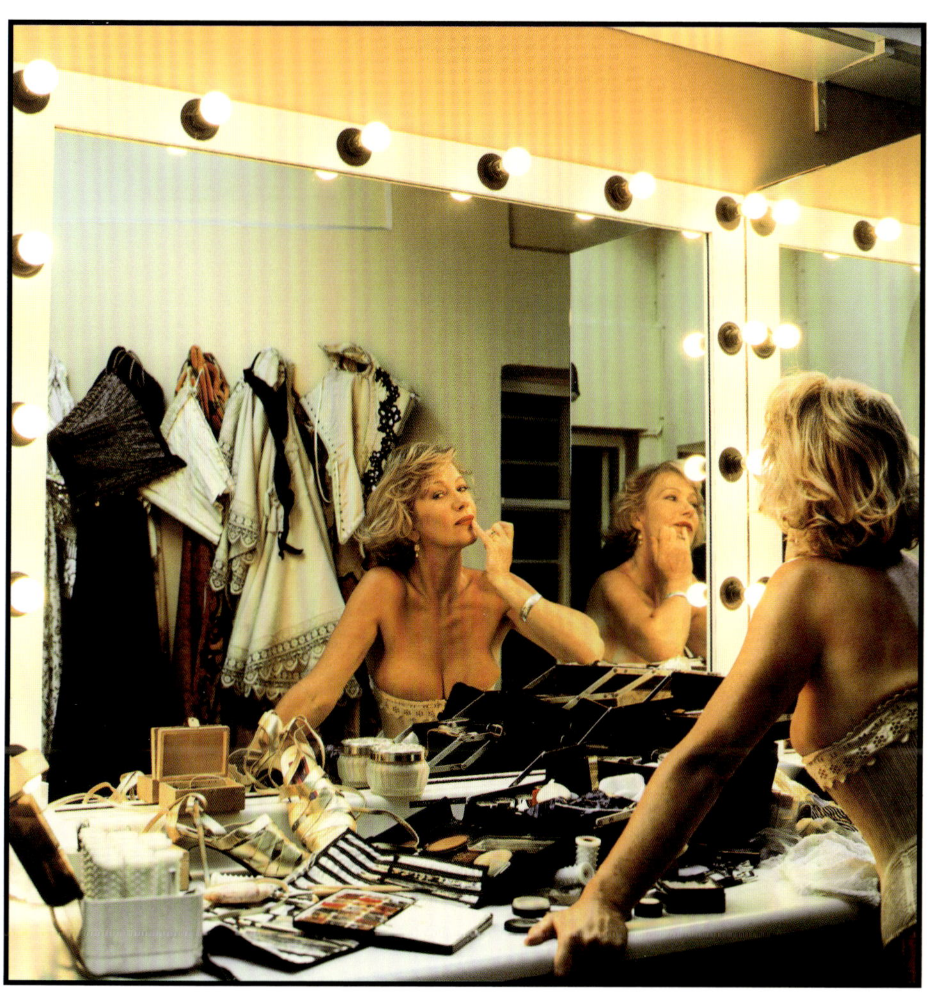

66
—

HELEN MIRREN
1995

78

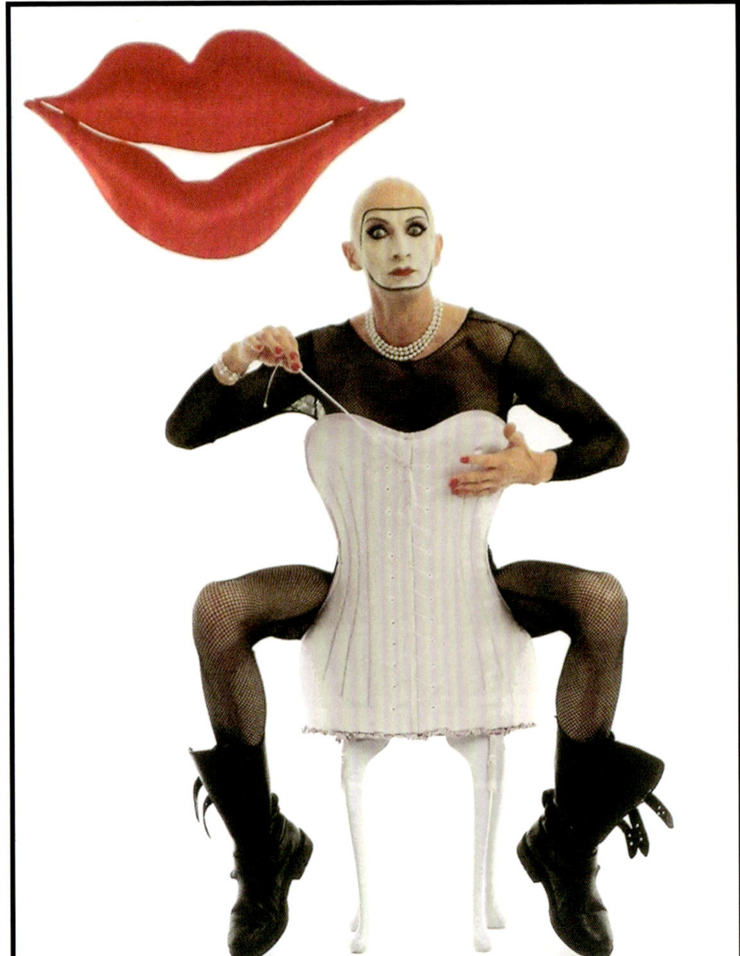

67
—
RICHARD O'BRIEN
1995

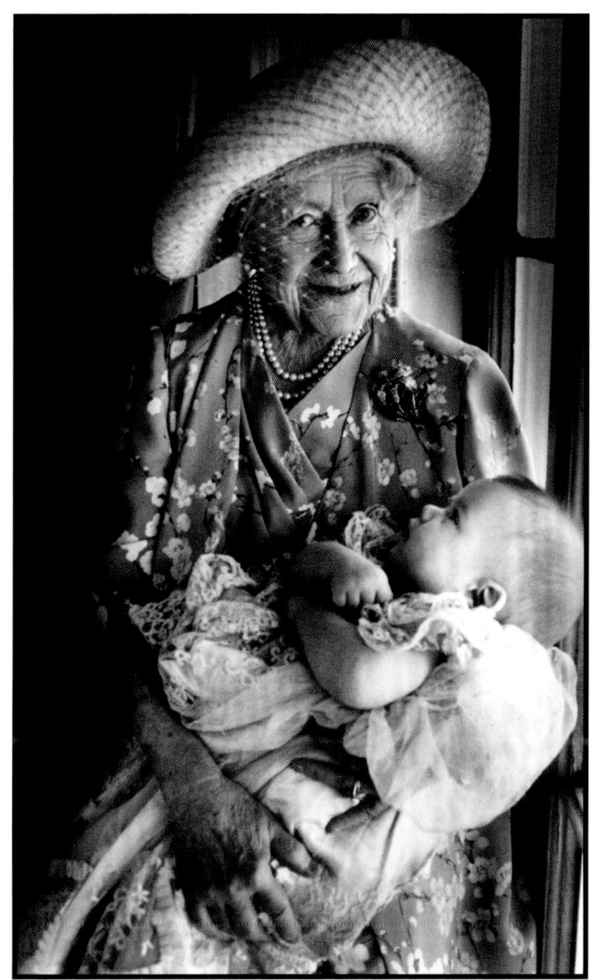

68

QUEEN ELIZABETH THE QUEEN MOTHER WITH HER GREAT-GRANDSON,
ARTHUR CHATTO, WINDSOR

1999

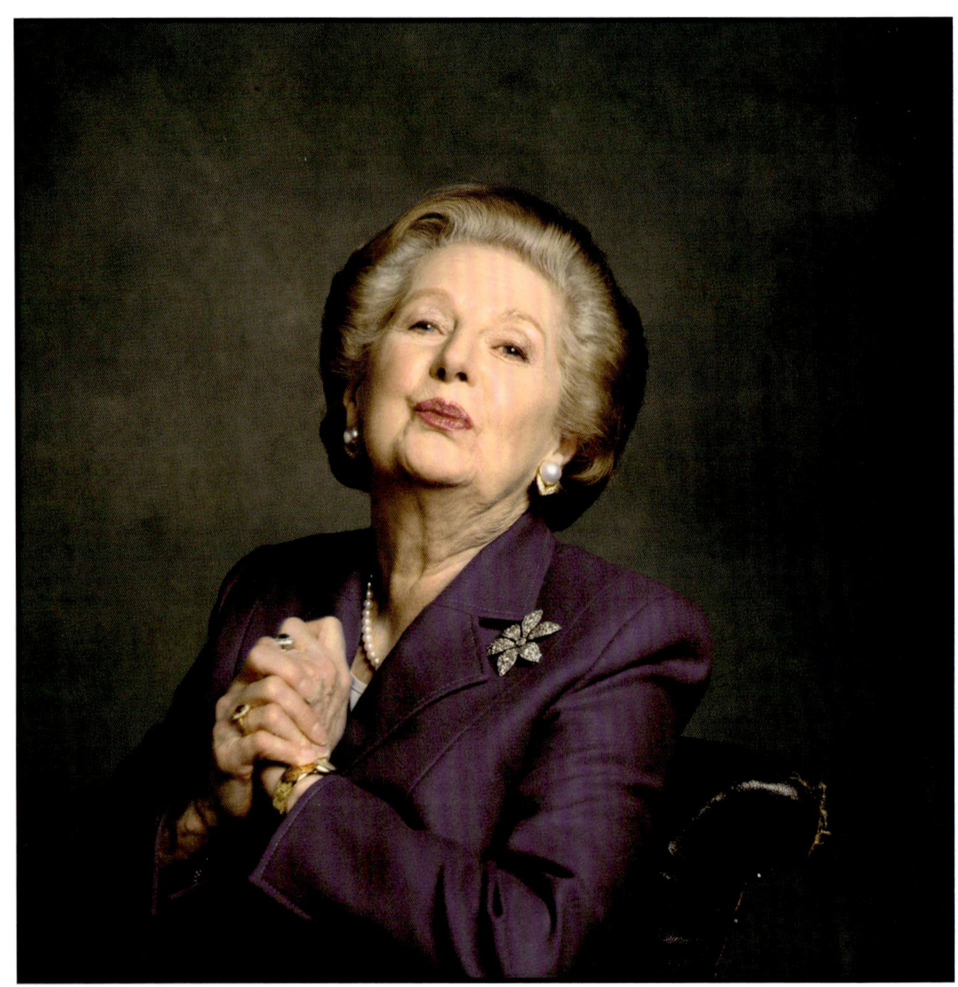

69

—

BARONESS THATCHER

2004

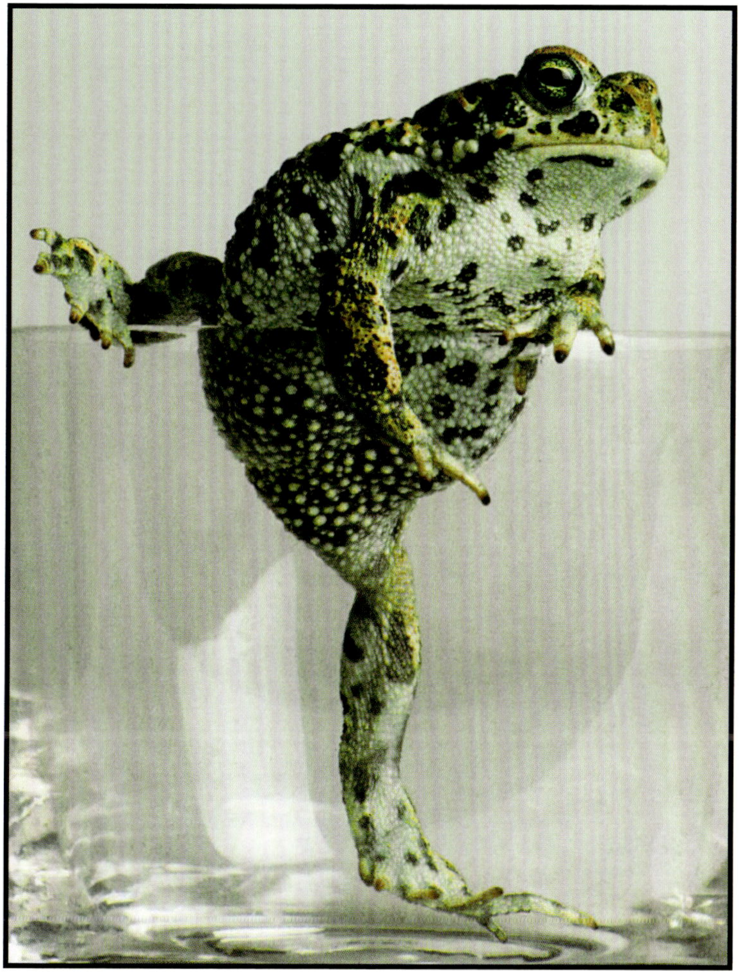

81

70

NATTERJACK TOAD
1985

LIST OF PLATES

All prints in the show are signed and numbered from strictly limited editions of 50,
controlled by Lord Snowdon and Chris Beetles Ltd

1 GLORIA CLARRY IN
A *TATLER* FASHION
SPREAD, *1955*
Hand printed on
silver gelatin paper
18 x 18 inches

2 GRETA WATSON IN
A *TATLER* FASHION
SPREAD, *1955*
Hand printed on
silver gelatin paper
18 x 18 inches

3 ADVERTISEMENT
FOR HAMLEY'S TOYS,
1956
Hand printed on
silver gelatin paper
18 x 18 inches

4 ROBIN TATERSAL IN
AN ADVERTISEMENT
FOR ACRILAN, *1957*
Hand printed on
silver gelatin paper
18 x 18 inches

5 ROBIN TATERSAL IN
AN ADVERTISEMENT
FOR ACRILAN, *1957*
Hand printed on
silver gelatin paper
18 x 18 inches

6 JEAN QUICK IN AN
ADVERTISEMENT FOR
COURTAULDS HATS,
1957
Hand printed on
silver gelatin paper
18 x 18 inches

7 ACRILAN
ADVERTISEMENT, *1957*
Hand printed on
silver gelatin paper
20 x 16.6

8 FASHION STILL,
JUNKYARD, QUEENS,
NEW YORK, *1957*
Hand printed on
silver gelatin paper
20 x 14 inches

9 SEKERS SILK
ADVERTISEMENT,
CERVINIA, ITALY, *1958*
Hand printed on
silver gelatin paper
18 x 18 inches

10 NANNIES ON ROTTEN
ROW, LONDON, *1958*
Hand printed on
silver gelatin paper
13½ x 20 inches

11 MR WILLIAM STONE
ALBANY, PICCADILLY,
LONDON, *1958*
Hand printed on
silver gelatin paper
20 x 16 inches

12 SUNDAY LUNCH AT
THE BRIDGEHOUSE
HOTEL, CANNING
TOWN, LONDON, *1958*
Hand printed on
silver gelatin paper
17¼ x 26 inches

13 THE LONDON STOCK
EXCHANGE, LONDON,
1958
Hand printed on
silver gelatin paper
17.5 x 20 inches

14 LAST DAY OF THE
CHELSEA FLOWER
SHOW, LONDON, *1958*
Hand printed on
silver gelatin paper
13½ x 20 inches

15 THE ETON AND
HARROW CRICKET
MATCH, LORDS,
LONDON, *1958*
Hand printed on
silver gelatin paper
20 x 13½ inches

16 TROOPING THE
COLOUR, LONDON,
1958
Hand printed on
silver gelatin paper
13½ x 20 inches

17 OLD AGE, *THE
SUNDAY TIMES
MAGAZINE, 1964*
Hand printed on
silver gelatin paper
13½ x 20 inches

18 SOME OF OUR
CHILDREN, *THE
SUNDAY TIMES
MAGAZINE, 1965*
Hand printed on
silver gelatin paper
20 x 13½ inches

19 LONELINESS (DEAF
MUTE IN BRIGHTON),
*THE SUNDAY TIMES
MAGAZINE, 1966*
Hand printed on
silver gelatin paper
20 x 13½ inches

20 MENTAL HOSPITALS
(PATIENT KNITTING),
*THE SUNDAY TIMES
MAGAZINE, 1968*
Hand printed on
silver gelatin paper
20 x 13½ inches

21 MENTAL HOSPITALS
(NURSE AND
PATIENT), *THE
SUNDAY TIMES
MAGAZINE, 1968*
Hand printed on
silver gelatin paper
13½ x 20 inches

22 CHILDREN UNDER
STRESS, *THE SUNDAY
TIMES MAGAZINE, 1970*
Hand printed on
silver gelatin paper
20 x 13½ inches

23 MONKEY SKINNING,
PERU, *1972*
Digitally printed on
c-type paper
21 x 13½ inches

24 CATACOMBS, PERU,
1972
Digitally printed on
c-type paper
20 x 13½ inches

25 NURSE AND
HYDROCEPHALIC
CHILD, *1975*
Hand printed on
silver gelatin paper
20 x 13½ inches

26 THE WAILING WALL,
JERUSALEM, *1985*
Hand printed on
silver gelatin paper
20 x 13½ inches

27 BERLIN WALL, *1986*
Hand printed on
silver gelatin paper
13½ x 20 inches

28 SVETLANA
BERIOSOVA IN JOHN
CRANKO'S *PRINCE OF
THE PAGODAS,*
COVENT GARDEN,
LONDON, *1956*
Hand printed on
silver gelatin paper
20 x 15.3 inches

29 LAURENCE OLIVIER
AS ARCHIE RICE IN
THE ENTERTAINER,
ROYAL COURT
THEATRE, LONDON,
1957
Hand printed on
silver gelatin paper
17.6 x 20 inches

30 PAUL SCOFIELD IN
*THE POWER AND
THE GLORY,* ROYAL
COURT THEATRE,
LONDON, *1957*
Hand printed on
silver gelatin paper
20 x 14.2 inches

31 FONTEYN & NUREYEV
REHEARSING
*MARGUERITE AND
ARMAND,* ROYAL
BALLET SCHOOL,
LONDON, *1963*
Hand printed on silver
gelatin paper
20 x 13½ inches

32 STUDENT AT THE
VAGANOVA SCHOOL,
ST PETERSBURG, *2002*
Hand printed on
silver gelatin paper
13½ x 20 inches

33 MARLENE DIETRICH,
THE CAFE DE PARIS,
LONDON, *1955*
Hand printed on
silver gelatin paper
18 x 18 inches

34 BRENDAN BEHAN,
DUBLIN, *1957*
Hand printed on
silver gelatin paper
18 x 18 inches

35 BABE PALEY, NEW
YORK CITY, *1958*
Hand printed on
silver gelatin paper
18 x 18 inches